It's all Good

D1420069

It's all Good

HOW TO TRUST AND SURRENDER TO THE BIGGER PLAN

CASSIE MENDOZA-JONES

HAY HOUSE

Carlsbad, California • New York City • London
Sydney • Johannesburg • Vancouver • New Delhi

First published and distributed in the United Kingdom by:
Hay House UK Ltd, Astley House, 33 Notting Hill Gate, London W11 3JQ
Tel: +44 (0)20 3675 2450; Fax: +44 (0)20 3675 2451; www.hayhouse.co.uk

Published and distributed in the United States of America by:
Hay House Inc., PO Box 5100, Carlsbad, CA 92018-5100
Tel: (1) 760 431 7695 or (800) 654 5126
Fax: (1) 760 431 6948 or (800) 650 5115; www.hayhouse.com

Published and distributed in Australia by:
Hay House Australia Ltd, 18/36 Ralph St, Alexandria NSW 2015
Tel: (61) 2 9669 4299; Fax: (61) 2 9669 4144; www.hayhouse.com.au

Published and distributed in the Republic of South Africa by:
Hay House SA (Pty) Ltd, PO Box 990, Witkoppen 2068
info@hayhouse.co.za; www.hayhouse.co.za

Published and distributed in India by:
Hay House Publishers India, Muskaan Complex, Plot No.3, B-2,
Vasant Kunj, New Delhi 110 070
Tel: (91) 11 4176 1620; Fax: (91) 11 4176 1630; www.hayhouse.co.in

Distributed in Canada by:
Raincoast Books, 2440 Viking Way, Richmond, B.C. V6V 1N2
Tel: (1) 604 448 7100; Fax: (1) 604 270 7161; www.raincoast.com

Copyright © 2017 by Cassie Mendoza-Jones

The moral rights of the author have been asserted.

Cover Design by Neverland Studio; Internal Design by Rhett Nacson; Typeset by Bookhouse;
Author photo by Bayleigh Vedelago; Edited by Margie Tubb

All rights reserved. No part of this book may be reproduced by any mechanical, photographic or
electronic process, or in the form of a phonographic recording; nor may it be stored in a retrieval
system, transmitted or otherwise be copied for public or private use, other than for 'fair use' as brief
quotations embodied in articles and reviews, without prior written permission of the publisher.

The information given in this book should not be treated as a substitute for professional medical
advice; always consult a medical practitioner. Any use of information in this book is at the reader's
discretion and risk. Neither the author nor the publisher can be held responsible for any loss, claim
or damage arising out of the use, or misuse, of the suggestions made, the failure to take medical
advice or for any material on third party websites.

A catalogue record for this book is available from the British Library.

ISBN: 978-1-78180-989-1

Printed in Great Britain by CPI Group (UK) Ltd, Croydon CR0 4YY

To you, my reader, for being brave enough to pick yourself up, to try again, and to trust it's all worth it.

Here's to the bitter sweetness of failure, the delightfulness of clarity, the rush of new beginnings and the gratitude of rebirths.

CONTENTS

Introduction   ix

part 1 THE END

chapter 1   What's All Good?   3
chapter 2   The Adventure that Got Us Here   9
chapter 3   Liberate Your Expectations   18
chapter 4   Be Proud   25
chapter 5   The Best Things   28
chapter 6   We Are the Masters   37
chapter 7   Your Perception Is Everything   44
chapter 8   Your Failure Can Be Your Progression   53
chapter 9   The Fear of It   59
chapter 10 Keep the Golden Nugget   62
chapter 11 A Bone to Pick   71
chapter 12 We Grow by Letting Go   74
chapter 13 Your Compass Back Home   81
chapter 14 Dive Underneath   86
chapter 15 Feeling Good   100
chapter 16 Change Your Tune   107
chapter 17 Bend or Break   111

part 2 THE MIDDLE

chapter 18 There's a New Map   117
chapter 19 Bravo, Bravo!   125
chapter 20 Sweet, Sweet Clarity   128

chapter 21   Lead from Your Heart   136

chapter 22   The Space between Dreams and Goals   144

chapter 23   It's Okay to Change   152

chapter 24   Compassion Prevails   157

chapter 25   Your River Is Different Now   162

chapter 26   The Path of Ascension   170

chapter 27   Turn the Lights On   175

chapter 28   The Pilot and the Jelly   179

chapter 29   You Are Safe   187

chapter 30   It's the Glue that Keeps You Together   196

part3   THE BEGINNING

chapter 31   The Current of Your Life   205

chapter 32   Synchronicity and Serendipity   213

chapter 33   Be Here Now   217

chapter 34   The Love Story of You and You   223

chapter 35   Going Inwards   226

chapter 36   Plugging into Your Power   231

chapter 37   Or Something Better?   236

chapter 38   Dance with Change   252

chapter 39   This Is Your Journey, After All   255

Compendium   259

Recapped   263

A Note to My Reader   265

Connect with Cass   267

Acknowledgments   268

About the Author   271

INTRODUCTION

There's a riddle I used to love when I was younger: a man is in a room with no doors and no windows. All he has are two halves of a table, an apple, a piece of string, a chair, some nails and a hammer (or some such random combination).

— The riddle?   How does he get out?
— The answer?   He nails the table back together, so the two halves become a whole. And then … he crawls out of the hole!

Okay … that makes no logical (or grammatical) sense. And yes, 'hole' should be 'whole'—hence the resolution of this conundrum. But, see what he did there? He shifted his mindset. He got out of his own way. He didn't call himself a failure. He didn't spend time wondering about how he got there. He created a solution out of a problem. He ignored the things he didn't need (the apple, the chair, the string) and used the tools that would make all the difference.

And … he got out. (So basically, he's MacGyver.)

If you've picked up this book, perhaps there's an element of your life that's making you feel as though you are trapped in a room too, with just an assortment of random tools and no clear doorway out. Maybe things in your life are feeling stuck and stagnant, so dark that you can't even see your hand when you hold it out in front of your face. Maybe you think you've failed. Maybe it's feeling increasingly harder and harder to get back into your flow, to find your momentum again, to feel like you're on the right track.

Maybe things are feeling so dire, so uncomfortable and so heavy that you feel you're at your wit's end, and you just need a break. Have you been searching for the answer, for the solution, for a way out of this confusion? Or perhaps you're near the end of what has felt like an impossible and difficult journey, and you're finding it hard to let go of what you've been through, so that you can move on and move up.

I know how you feel, because I've been on this journey too. This journey of wading through muck and confusion, wondering why things weren't going the way I wanted them to. I've been through the challenge of finding it so hard to maintain the balance between setting beautiful and flowing intentions and goals, yet realising I had high and rigid expectations of their outcomes. I've also at times felt stuck in that place between setting your goals and seeing your dreams turn into reality (or something better), wanting to rush the process along, feeling impatient and ungrounded, all the while knowing that if I just allowed myself to be happy with where I was, I would actually enjoy the process of growth and change (instead of fighting against it).

And—perhaps most importantly—I've been through the journey of learning how to stay open, ready and able to receive the shift I needed. I've learnt to recognise when the time became right for me to acknowledge and make use of the inner resilience and resourcefulness that was already mine, and to forgive myself for my perceived failures and for all the things I thought I was lacking, in order to get back up, dust myself off and, as the saying goes: *Try, try again.*

I've been there. Oh gosh, how I've been there! And I know this: no matter where you are on your journey, the next step you must take is to trust that everything will be okay. If life has felt a little harsh lately, believe that what you're going through will not last forever. Trust that you're learning lessons you'll use again and again later on, and trust that when all is said and done, it's all good and everything will be okay.

When I was midway through this journey for myself, I remember wondering if one of the many books on my bookshelf could shed some light on what I was feeling, and how to move forwards. So I searched for a book that would soothe my soul, show me how to surrender, and say to me: 'It's all good. Everything is going to be okay.' This searching didn't come from a desire to seek external validation—this came from a desire for someone else to be a witness to my pain and my journey, and for me to be a witness to someone else's, so that I could know I wasn't alone in what I was feeling.

And then one day, after days of feeling stuck, and after still not having found the book I was looking for, I received an intuitive hit—soft at first, and stronger as the days and weeks went by. It said: 'You'll get through this Cass, and then you'll write that book yourself.' Even though I had been feeling stuck for so long, even though I couldn't see how I would move forwards (yet), the intuitive hit felt so right, and I knew it to be true. The feeling was almost a knowing that the lessons I was learning were so much bigger than I was. I survived all of it, and so will you.

And so, here we are. It's my hope that this book will provide the same for you in reading it, as it did for me in living it, and writing it: hope, a guiding light, a pathway through darkness (or even just a very dim corridor) and confirmation that you are not alone—that I see you, and you see me. It's my hope that when you read this book, you're reminded that you truly are on the right path, that you really are doing the right thing, that you are stronger and more resilient than you know, and that it's all good; everything will be okay.

— This book is about: —

— Releasing and making peace with any past disappointments
— Letting go of your perceived failures, getting back up after a fall, dusting yourself off and trying again
— Surrendering to where you're at, so you can rise above it
— Finding strength and courage to show up in your life again after a disappointment, as your best self
— Letting go of expectations, while still setting goals and intentions, and being more than okay to sit in those spaces between setting your goals and seeing your dreams manifest
— Taking aligned action in your life, without attaching, controlling or making yourself suffer through hard times,

and without gripping so tightly that you lose touch with yourself in the process

— Giving yourself permission to find new ground after a failure, instead of feeling like you're just grasping at straws

— Acknowledging that the hard moments are so often the ones that teach you the most (ah, hindsight, you can be so beautiful!)

— Backing yourself (and coming back to yourself) even if things feel hard, even if things don't turn out how you'd like, and even if you're not sure of the outcome

— Aligning to manifesting without expectations, and to receiving what you desire (or something better)

In this book, you'll be able to start opening yourself up to a new way of thinking and being. And while I'll certainly guide you on where to take action as and where and when it's needed, that's only half the story.

The rest of the story comes from you—it comes from inside you and above you. It comes from just out of your reach, to just below your feet. It's an energy and a feeling, a whisper that you don't always catch. It's letting go of where you think you should be, so you can arrive at where you need to be.

Surrendering isn't tangible, which is why we often try to hold on and control it with all our might. Through these chapters, you'll see and feel and realise that surrendering to where you are is easier, not because you're giving up but because that's how you can then step up in your life. You'll see that letting go can invite in freedom, not fear. It can feel natural and easy and wonderful. There is something within each of us that deeply wants us to surrender. And even though our ego so often wants us to grip ... we are strong enough to let go.

You are strong enough to surrender. You are capable of aligning to your inner wisdom, to your soul, to the part of you who doesn't mind if you think you've succeeded, or if you fear you've failed—the part of you who knows and trusts that everything will be okay.

You are resilient enough to become truly aligned to who you are through your challenges and beyond, to living your purpose, to living on purpose (no matter how many times you fall along the way).

So ... that's what this book is about. I want to help you realise, feel and understand how to surrender to where you are, how to flow, and how to shift your energy and your mindset, without always fighting with forces outside of your control.

I so hope you'll join me on this journey. It's an important one. And here's something I know, something I can share in a titbit now, and will share in more detail throughout the pages of this book: if you try to force this process, it won't feel good.

If you don't take this journey when the time is right— when you really need to for your highest good and growth—it might catch up with you later. That isn't a scary threat. It's just the honest truth. (Well, a truth I've experienced, anyway.)

Sometimes we want to start the journey before we're ready, but not this one. You can't force this process. But one day, when you realise you're ready to start surrendering to where you are, to start accepting your journey for all it's been and for all it is, then you'll know you're ready. And if you're ready, come with me.

Just like the man in the riddle, you can create a whole (or a hole!) out of parts, you can put things back together, and you can climb out of the darkness and into the light. You can move from feeling stuck, to feeling in the flow.

If you're ready to start trusting, and if you're ready to let go of your expectations so that you can feel deeply supported and be beautifully surprised and lifted up by life, then let's get going, shall we?

— **How to work with the affirmations
and meditations in this book** —

At the end of most chapters, you'll either find some affirmations you may wish to work with, a short meditation, or some kind of self-trust activity that is helpful for you to take yourself through, in order to move through this process of surrendering to where you are, and of trusting the bigger plan.

I gently urge you to not skip through any of the healing exercises, because cutting corners won't help you get to the finishing line faster. (Probably because, in this case, there is no finishing line.)

The best and easiest way to work with the affirmations is in any way that feels good to you!

Here are some ideas:

— Simply place your hands over your heart and read them to yourself, taking a deep breath in and out.

— Use them as journaling prompts.

— Use them as mantras or affirmations each morning or evening, or during meditation or yoga.

— Choose a few and set them as daily reminders on your phone or in your calendar.

— Write them out on post-its and stick them where you'll see them daily.

— Make art out of them; sit down with a blank piece of paper and draw what feels like the essence of the meditation or the affirmation of your choice. Maybe it will turn into a beautiful mandala or pattern, or perhaps a postcard that you can send to a friend (or to yourself).

Okay. Ready when you are.

— Go with the Flow Affirmation —

If you'll forgive me for quoting myself, I'd love to offer you my *Go with the Flow Affirmation*, taken directly from my book, *You Are Enough*. Read it over and absorb it, before diving into Chapter 1.

In real time as I write this, just a few days ago I received an email from a young woman who told me that she reads this particular affirmation to herself every morning before she starts her day. She told me that it has helped her profoundly to stay present, feel calmer, and become more forgiving towards and accepting of herself. I hope you find it helpful too.

So … here you go. Deep breath in.

The Go with the Flow Affirmation

I surrender.

I let go.

I trust I'm exactly where I'm supposed to be.

I know that trusting this will allow me to feel
more connected, guided, supported and grounded,
and I know I'm being guided on my current path,
because this is the right path for me to be on.

I'm aligned to my growth and transformation in whichever
way betters me for my highest good. I let go of all that
no longer serves me. It's safe for me to let things be
easy. It's easy for me to let things go with the flow.

I love and forgive myself.

I surrender. I let go. I know I'm exactly
where I'm supposed to be.

I allow the flow to take me where I need to go.

I surrender.

I let go.

You might like to say this affirmation to yourself each
morning and night, for as long as feels right to you. You
may also choose to write down some reflections about how
you're feeling before, or free write in your journal afterwards.
Whatever comes up is perfect for you, and will be healing on
some level (oftentimes on more than one level).

YOU MIGHT HAVE WOUNDS TO LICK,

BUT THE SCARS WILL TELL STORIES

YOU'LL WANT TO REMEMBER.

#itsallgoodbook

part 1

THE END

AFTER YOUR FAILURE

---

chapter 1

WHAT'S ALL GOOD?

———

*B*efore we dive in, I want to clarify something. Throughout this book, I'll say a variation of 'it's all good' or 'everything will be okay' quite a few times, because it's true and I mean it. When I say this, I'm not trying to be condescending. I'm not trying to make you ignore the challenges you might have recently gone through or the ones you may be going through now; and I certainly don't mean we must sugar-coat the hard times, those times we feel particularly fearful because we don't know what the outcome or ending will be.

When I say 'it's all good' or 'everything will be okay' or 'trust where you are right now' or any variation of those phrases, I mean that we must trust, show up and surrender to where we are anyway—even if it feels hard, even if we don't always feel like we know where we're going, even if we feel scared that we may be doing the wrong thing. We must trust—even if we think we might fail (again, or for the first time) and even if we wonder if it's all going to be worth it.

We must trust that things will turn out the way they are supposed to, and that we will be okay in the end.

We must trust that we are strong enough to make it through (or over, or under) the obstacles in our path, to ride through the challenges we face, to step over the demons into whose eyes we look.

We must trust that if it feels like we've suddenly found ourselves in a dark corridor, with our old path's door slammed shut behind us and a new door not yet in our reach, we **can** take one step forward and then another, and we can do this again and again until our hand reaches the doorhandle that opens into to the next phase of our lives. We must trust that just because we can't see the new door, that doesn't mean it doesn't exist. It doesn't mean we're on the wrong path. It doesn't mean we won't find our next door.

We must trust … because to not trust is to overthink, to worry, and to be constantly fearful and anxious. To not trust is to play small in our own lives.

No matter what you go through in the future, or what you're going through now, trust yourself that you can get through it.

You can get through it.

And trust that afterwards—when the obstacle is in your past and the pain is in your shadow as you walk away from it—you will still love and be loved.

After the pain, the lessons, the integration and the insight, you will still be worthy, and you will be even stronger. You will be more grounded in your truth. You might even have a new truth to stand for. You will be here. You will still be enough. **You will always be enough.**

You might be a little more bruised (the bruises will fade, the pain will heal), but you will be so much wiser (and this wisdom will last). You might have wounds to lick, but the scars will tell stories you'll want to remember.

For a little while, you might wonder why the stories had to hurt. But you'll see the lessons and the greatness and the strength in them, and in yourself too. Importantly, you'll be okay. You will be okay.

Trusting that everything will be okay is about surrendering, trusting, and then surrendering and trusting some more.

Believing that everything will be okay is about letting go of the veils of illusion, so that we don't lean into fear, but we lean into trust. Another of those veils we must let go of is the whisper that says: 'You have to have all the answers and all your ducks in a row before you can take your next step.' Let me tell you—you don't. You can find your way as you make your way. You can decide where to walk as you pick one foot up and place it in front of the other. You can take baby steps every day, and they can take you so very far.

Through failing and picking myself up again and again, I've learnt a few great truths. You might not have all the puzzle pieces yet, but that doesn't mean you can't begin (again).

You might not have all your puzzle pieces, but that doesn't mean you can't still see the bigger picture: the greater vision of your life, the place where your dreams have landed and where your soul says: 'Yes! This is where you were always headed.'

Even on the days where your vision of your future feels foggy, and you can't muster the strength to wipe the tears and the fears away, trust anyway. Trust that you will be okay in the end.

Knowing that everything will be okay is about taking action once you've picked yourself up after a failure or a disappointment, then opening up to create and receive what you desire (or, as we'll explore towards the end of this book, creation through intention and receiving) or something better, all the while releasing expectations, showing up and knowing it's all worth it (even the really hard moments, and the really hard days, and the really hard weeks).

Being in a space of trust and surrender doesn't necessarily mean the hard moments feel any less hard; it means you know you have the strength, resilience and self-compassion to move through them anyway. It means you know you're in the right place, right now.

So, is this book (and the process of surrendering) simply about letting everything go and just seeing what comes next? Well, yes and no. Yes, if you're ready to approach life with an open heart, mind and soul, taking action and showing up for yourself every day. But no, not if you're doing this to spite yourself.

Trusting isn't about testing yourself or the universe. Trusting is about aligning, opening up to guidance (of the inner and higher varieties) and being 'all in', no matter what. Trusting is about being in your body, and not always (or only sometimes) in your head. It's about believing that you are supported and knowing that, on some level, that glorious vision you hold for your life is already written in the stars (with a generous side dish of free will and a deep desire to create a beautiful life).

You're about to take a deep dive into the flowing (and sometimes floundering) process of surrendering and showing up, no matter how fearful, hurt or unsure you are. Just because working towards your dreams and goals to create the life you want to lead, live and love doesn't always feel like it's an easy, flowing ride, doesn't mean you're on the wrong path.

Who ever said creating your best life and being the very best version of yourself was going to be a cakewalk? No-one ever. But this doesn't mean you can't create your very best life, and be the very best version of yourself anyway.

The process of surrendering doesn't always feel like a 'process' either, with a storybook beginning, middle and end. And honestly, for me it's never really felt that it works that way. Even so, it **is** a process and hence the three parts of this book, starting at the end and ending at the beginning.

Surrendering and trusting is within your reach, and when you look within, you'll see you already know how to trust, how to surrender to where you are, and how to show up for yourself, again and again and again.

I think our best lives are sitting beneath the surface of what we're trying to control and micromanage. I think the challenging, difficult and trying times are the times when we learn, grow and expand the most.

Our failures can show us what we're made of, and teach us to love and honour ourselves more deeply, if only we'd give them the chance. I believe that when we can trust our journey and let go of what we no longer need, then we can truly come up for air, with a new-found ability to approach our lives with a fresh perspective; one that stems from resilience, and a devotion to our dreams.

— Take a breath —

Before we dive into the next chapter, take a moment, a pause, a breath, and let yourself be here right now—in this book, in this moment; in your body, your skin, your breath and your life. Take a moment to be here, all here, now.

See how you're okay? Right now, at this very moment, you are okay. Which means you can be okay for all the moments to come as well. It means you can be more than okay. It means you can live freely, fully, wildly and boldly (and also comfortably and Netflix-and-chilled-ly).

Even if things aren't the way you want them to be, you are okay, right now. Even if you feel sad, you are okay, right now. Even if you feel scared, you are okay, right now.

Take a deep breath in and a long, slow breath out.

Don't underestimate the power of your breath to bring you back here, into this moment, where you are safe and loved and held and okay.

Don't underestimate the power of you, to bring you back here, into this moment, where you are safe and loved and held and okay.

chapter 2

THE ADVENTURE
THAT GOT US HERE

———

What we call the beginning is often the end.
And to make an end is to make a beginning.
The end is where we start from.

T.S. ELIOT

I'm going to explain the story behind this book as
succinctly as I can, not because it's not important (it
obviously is) and not because I don't want you to know the
details (I obviously do) but because I'm acutely aware that my
story is so personal—so much a part of my inner workings—
and I want you to be able to see the universal themes that
weave through it, so that this book can resonate easily and
strongly with you, and make up part of your support system
when you need it most.

I'm also aware that my story—the journey to writing this
book—was seeded in my business, but I know you don't need
to run your own business to be called to surrender, to wake
up from a failure and see it as a great lesson, or to find your

new ground and arrive at a new way of being, of seeing, of doing things. My business—and a particular project—was the vessel for my lesson, my change, my apprenticeship to surrendering and letting go, as well as my soul growth. But the lessons are universal.

This journey began several years ago, when I had an incredibly successful year in my business. It felt like all my hard work was paying off; it felt like I was finally getting to where I wanted to be (wherever 'there' is). I was feeling so confident, grateful and happy. I felt fully in my flow, receptive and open to things flowing to me, being guided by my intuition. I could feel that expansion was not just happening at the time, but that more and more of it was on its way to me. (Ah, hindsight now tells me that to kick off this expansion, the ground beneath my feet had to rumble and shift and shake until I fell to my knees, many times.)

I felt abundant, visible and supported. Things in my personal life were also wonderful. Life was really, really good.

Underneath all of this external success was a desire to keep moving forward towards more growth in my business. I also wanted to expand my offerings and shift slightly out of my current business model, which was mostly seeing private clients, with some digital products always available for purchase on my website, and a few launches of bigger eCourses each year.

I loved working in this way, but I also wanted to take my business to a new level of abundance and visibility and felt that more online offerings would help me do this. I'd been having great success with online courses, so this felt like a natural step for me.

So my big, expansive idea dropped in—the idea I envisioned would take me to that 'next level' in my business—and I went to work on this massive project. This was the project I thought would be my next big thing, not just because of how it would serve and support my clients and readers, but also because of how amazing it felt to create. It felt so right because of how much I loved doing the work on it, and because I felt so aligned and in tune with it, as if this was exactly where I was supposed to be (because, as I learnt, it was exactly where I was supposed to be!).

I worked on it solidly for months, almost a year in fact. I put so much into it: time, energy, money, resources, as well as so much love and pure intention. It was the main focus of my business, perhaps even my life, for many months.

But it didn't work out the way I had planned.

The thing is, after the tens of thousands of dollars I put into this new project (getting myself into debt along the way); after months and months of hard work; after expanding my business support team from two to six people; after upgrading all of my systems and processes; after effectively managing all the problems that inevitably crop up in a months-long, web-based development project; after an unexpected legal issue popping up eight days before launch that necessitated adding a team of lawyers into the mix, renaming the project, redoing the website and branding, adjusting the content and graphics and pushing the launch back by a month … the project just didn't take off the way I'd expected it to.

I can't say it was a flop, but it didn't feel like a 'success' in the way I'd envisioned it. The initial outcome didn't match what I'd put in. To me, it felt like it wasn't energetically adding up. From the week of the launch, I felt like something was off—something I couldn't quite put my finger on. With hindsight, I can see that I had placed too much value—too much of my self-worth—into this project. When the project seemed to fail, I felt like I had failed. When the project didn't seem to be a success, I felt like I wasn't a success. When the project seemed to take more from me than it gave back, I felt like I had nothing left to give.

In the months that followed, I felt confused, hurt and sometimes angry. I wanted to shrink and to hide. I wanted to go back and do things differently. How could I have put so much effort into this project, and not receive the same amount of energy back? And why wasn't it going where I wanted it to? What had I done wrong?

And how could anything have gone 'wrong' when it had felt so right for so long?

Basically, I experienced a failure (that wasn't a failure at all, as the lessons later taught me) and I felt defeated. I had challenged myself in so many ways, and I'd had the highest expectations of myself and my project. I had put so much in, and expected too much in return. I'd thought that because I'd put so much love into it, I'd receive that back, or more. I'd thought that because I tried so hard, it would all work out, exactly as I'd planned. (Coming to terms with that belief was one of the greatest lessons I learnt, and one of the experiences I had to heal from the most.)

Put simply, I'd had expectations and I'd been disappointed.

I grieved. I felt sad. I felt stuck. I got sick, twice in several months (all lung stuff—letting go, and processing guilt, grief and regret). I had to take time off work and do a lot of clearing and healing on a physical level. This was coming through because I thought I'd failed, and I wasn't letting it go on a very deep level. I was giving myself a really hard time about it.

I was sure things in my business would never be the same. I felt anxious and small, invisible and unimportant. I remember thinking I would never get out of debt.

I even remember looking for other jobs online, thinking about what else I could do for work, then feeling guilty about it—not that there's anything wrong with opening up to more support while you build your business. There were brief moments where I seriously considered throwing in the towel with my business.

(Side note: I've secretly always wanted to be in the FBI or CIA, even though that's impossible because I'm not a US citizen so I'm not eligible—I love how I've even looked that up—but even if I was, I couldn't tell you that otherwise I'd have to … oh wait. Never mind, forget I said anything. Look, Beyoncé!)

Looking back, I think maybe this was my rock bottom. Maybe I am a high-functioning rock bottomer, as most people in my life wouldn't have known I was bottoming out. Not because I made huge attempts to hide this from people, but more because it was such a silent (okay, sometimes not so silent), internal battle. It was a rumbling of my soul and my energy, a stirring that said: 'Okay, so things didn't turn out as you expected them to. What are you going to do now? You have to clear this first, and then you have more places to go, more to be. There is more … and you are not quite there yet.'

— Spaces in between —

It's often said that your best ideas come to you in the spaces in between, and I wholeheartedly agree. Except that this period of my life also felt like a 'space in between', one that fit in a space that held both dreams and failures, but which didn't hold the new vision for my future just yet. This experience was teaching me to trust in those spaces in between.

For a while there, it didn't feel as though my best ideas were coming to me. My vision was foggy: spiritually, mentally, and emotionally. It felt like the end, but I couldn't see the new beginning yet. Emotionally, I felt like I was all over the place.

I also started to doubt myself, my intuition and my decisions. This had all felt so **right**. How had it gone so **wrong**?

The very dazzling truth was that I couldn't see the truth yet. I couldn't see the woods for the trees—that higher perspective I so needed time to see. I just saw the insular version that hadn't worked out the way I'd wanted it to in my mind. I was looking at my situation from one side, one angle. It took me months (and so much inner work, clearing and healing) to walk around it and see it from all angles; to see that everything was okay, to see that I'd done an incredible job, and to see that it was all worth it—not in spite of every confusing and painful lesson I'd gone through, but because of those lessons.

I almost want to say I wish I'd gotten over it all really quickly but, as I started typing those words, I realised how silly that would sound. I am so grateful for the entire experience, because of the many lessons I learnt that I'll now take you through. Because if I hadn't gone through it all then, I wouldn't be writing this book now. Perhaps most importantly, if I hadn't gone through it all, I wouldn't be who I am right now.

My failure was the catalyst for my change, for my growth, and for my expansion. It was a reminder that we mustn't give up at the first (or second or third or fourth) hurdle. It was a reminder to keep expectations in check, to set clear intentions with breathing room, to open up to receive our intentions or something better. And it was a reminder that it's so very possible to release disappointment.

It was a reminder that after a perceived failure, **you will be okay.** You won't stay stagnant or stuck forever (even if it sometimes feels that way). You won't even be disappointed forever (even if it sometimes feels that way). Momentum will find you again because you'll create it yourself, when you've healed, and when you make space for it (even if it feels like you never will).

When you are ready, you will rise again. And most likely, you will be more aware, more sensitive to your own needs, and kinder to yourself. For me, it was a massive and beautiful initiation into surrendering, letting go of expectations, and making space to slow down and tap into a much more grounded, feminine way of being and working, right when I needed it the most. It was an initiation into a way of being that invites us to hustle less (yet magically, more seems to get done), to be, to find our flow and our earth, and to stay rooted in it.

There were so many ways out of where I found myself, but the path always began with a step into surrender. At first, I tried really hard to find another way: *Maybe I can just do more stuff, more things, more and more. Maybe there's another way out! Surely I don't have to let go or surrender to where I am. Surely there must be an easier way?*

Well, for me at least, there was no other way to begin but to surrender, to let go, and to make space for my new flow—a raised vibration, a new perspective, an expanded sense of self and a more resilient attitude. In order to move forwards, the hardest and easiest thing I could do was to surrender to where I was. And when I did finally surrender, I found more ease than I could have ever expected.

— What are you carrying? —

We all have a story. Sometimes it sits at the top of our being and we write our daily script using past stories, because we think we know how it's all going to play out. Sometimes we get so tangled up in our storyline that we forget to see our cue to exit. Sometimes we have no idea we're being run by our story. And so of course, to start this journey to surrender, you have to know your starting point.

Let's start at your beginning (or the end, after your failure). Where are you now? Where have you been? What are you feeling and holding onto? Take a breath, then take a moment to tune into what you're carrying with you. Is it disappointment, regret, a story of failure and misfortune?

If so, that's okay. Let yourself feel it all, carry it all. Before we begin to clear it, I invite you to do something with that energy: acknowledge it, see it and honour it.

Maybe you'll breathe it out in a strong and deep exhale. Maybe you'll grab your journal and write it all out, or go for a run around the block, release your tears, scream into a pillow, dance and shake it out, meditate for a few moments, or do anything else you feel you need.

Now, set an intention for how you'd like to feel throughout this journey of clearing, of surrendering, of trusting. It may be a word that comes to you, or several words, or a whole sentence.

Feel it all, the pain and the sadness, the fear and the stuckness—as much of it as you can—and now take another deep, cleansing breath in and out. Now, let's clear it all throughout the following pages.

***

The adventure that got you here affirmation

I am here now, and I am grateful for where I stand. I honour my journey so far, and give myself permission to take the next step forwards.

***

chapter 3

LIBERATE YOUR EXPECTATIONS

I think our stories can sometimes feel so painful because they don't match our expectations. I know that's definitely the case for me. If I hadn't had such great expectations, I would've had a completely different experience. But thinking like that doesn't actually help anyone. (I know because I thought like that for months, and it didn't get me anywhere!)

I know because when I felt stuck in the depths of my confusion, overwhelm and lack of momentum, I steeped and soaked and marinated in every other potential possibility of what might have happened ...

— if I'd thought it all through more
— if I hadn't spent so much money on the project
— if I was more successful
— if I'd gone into the project more slowly
— if I was stronger
— if I was smarter
— if I was easier on myself
— if I had been better at letting go

And on and on the inner dialogue went.

Do you find yourself going over and over past situations, then trying to reword them to fit a present or future that doesn't exist? Does it ever feel like it helps you move forwards, or is it a little like self-flagellation? Is it punishment because a part of you feels there's obviously something wrong with you, if you didn't create the perfect outcome?

This 'what-if' game doesn't support us in our journey of surrender and moving forward. In fact, it can keep us stuck. So, please give yourself permission to let go of your 'what-ifs'. It's a procrastination tactic that doesn't serve you.

We don't have a crystal ball (although if we did, I suppose all we'd see is pure possibility), and we can't be expected to anticipate the future. So instead we have to get ourselves out of the habit of creating rigid expectations that we think will get us there.

In fact, you wouldn't want to know your future. I know you're probably saying to yourself: 'Um, Cass, what are you talking about? Yes please, I'd love to know my future.' In a little while, I'll give you another angle that'll help you see that trusting your future is so much more beautiful than knowing it.

— What are expectations? —

Our expectations are the prospect of something great, of good fortune coming to us, of everything falling into place exactly as we imagined. They're our imagination out on a limb, crafting the golden outcome as we wait in anticipation, hoping that our wishes will come true. (And now! Pleeease!)

And if they don't come true as we'd imagined they would, we feel crushed, confused, at a loss. In fact, at a loss is exactly how I've felt so many times, when I've held incredibly high expectations of myself and of situations (and even of people). Then I've been left feeling thwarted in my attempts to craft this 'perfect' event or outcome.

It's easy to say, 'Oh, I'll just let go of my expectations.' But occasionally it feels as though we need them, right? Sometimes it feels like if we didn't create expectations and latch onto them tighter than a mollusc on an old shipwreck, our lives would fall apart, and then we'd have nothing to work towards.

How attached are you to the vision of your life that you dream about each day? What if something even better were around the corner, within your reach? All you have to do to see it is liberate your expectations—the sometimes inflexible assumptions you may have about what you should be doing in your life, and what should be happening for you.

The truth is so golden when we can flip that mindset on its head. You don't need to create expectations in order to reach your dreams and live out your fullest and most powerful potential. Sometimes it feels as though we create our expectations to feel like we belong to our dreams; but the truth is your dreams (even the ones you aren't aware of yet) are yours, whether you expect them to happen or not.

You can be your best self, and live your best life, without attaching to a perceived 'best' outcome, without micromanaging your outer world; and importantly, without giving yourself a hard time about what is or isn't happening for you on the timeline you've set for yourself.

— Crushed and confused —

I used to be very good at saying I didn't have expectations and then felt flattened when I didn't meet those secret, non-existent expectations. I'd find myself reeling, feeling crushed and confused. This has happened to me on and off throughout my life, teaching me lessons again and again.

Sometimes, during a period where we find ourselves finding it hard to surrender to where we are, and to forgive ourselves for being there, it can feel like a very drawn-out phase of our life. This doesn't mean it's actually a longer phase of our life, we just aren't enjoying it as much, so time seems to drag.

I felt this too. On some level, I knew it couldn't last forever, but it felt like it would. I wanted to move forwards so much, to put it all behind me, yet I was halting the flow by trying to force it. I just had to be in it, to go through it, to come out the other side of it.

My sense of failure seemed to heighten every other emotion I was feeling, and I really had to do a lot of inner work and clearing, in order to come back to myself in a grounded way.

Even though I was struggling to pick myself up from my perceived failures, after my incredibly high expectations hadn't landed where I'd wanted them to, there were still other areas of my life that felt like they were flowing (or at least, I wasn't in Struggle Town with them). Yet I wasn't focusing on those areas of my life that were working, flowing and feeling good. I had my blinkers on, and they were only directing me towards where I thought I'd gone wrong.

— Layers of failure —

When we go through a perceived failure, we find there are layers upon layers that the experience has created for us. Sometimes we must rifle through the complexity and the simplicity all in the same breath—the lessons and the insights and incredulously (after the initial confusion and head scratching), the dizzying growth, expansion, changes and integrations we have to go through (sometimes in almost every area of our lives), in order to step up and come back into our full power.

My 'business fail' was essentially the catalyst that took me on a massive journey. It required me to traverse not just my business landscape, but my home, personal, financial, social, family and inner landscapes too.

My failure asked me to stop placing my worth in external containers, and hold it within the vessel of myself instead. It asked me to scrap my old definition of success and rewrite a fresh one, so that in actual fact, my version of success needed nothing to do with the outside world and everything to do with how I feel in my innermost world.

It was a complete makeover. So even though it felt deep and dark sometimes, I can now say, 'Thank you, thank you.' And in a way, if I hadn't taken that journey (though not always willingly, mind you), this book wouldn't exist, and I might still be looking outside of myself for success, in all its forms.

— The moments we must traverse through —

There can be moments throughout really big difficulties where we can mistakenly think we'll never find the other side. Sometimes it takes hindsight to see how we got through it.

As Steve Jobs said, *You can't connect the dots looking forward. You can only connect them looking backwards. So you have to trust that the dots will somehow connect in your future.* When we're stuck in the energy of our problems, disappointments and difficulties, clearing them isn't always our first goal. We think it is, but truly we subconsciously want to escape the confusion of the energy in which we find ourselves.

To traverse the hardest moments, we have to step out of trying to be constantly solving and fixing the problem, and truly surrender to where we are. Then we can see everything with fresh eyes and clear energy. To quote the famous Albert Einstein: *No problem can be solved from the same level of consciousness that created it.*

When it comes to resolving difficulties and picking ourselves up after perceived pain and disappointment, escapism and resolution are not the same. Don't confuse them in your haste to make your problems disappear.

— **Crushed** —

Feeling crushed by our expectations is just one way we stop the flow of energy in our lives, which feeds into how we feel about ourselves, our actions and choices, our lives, and our life's vision and dreams.

We so often personify our expectations. We think about them and dream about them and scheme around them, until they feel like something that's part of us. If they don't turn out as we expected, it feels like a crushing and deeply personal blow.

We must transform the way we dream and 'attach' to events, expectations and outcomes. It's our own emotions around the expectations that get charged. Hence it's from within us that we can soften the anticipation, mould our ideas into something that feels and fits better, and release what's making us feel so reactive if things don't go our way.

What's so ironic when we're going through difficult periods in our lives is that they seem so difficult and so trying to us; yet if we were to tell our story to someone else, it may not seem like such a big deal to them. That's because our stories are what makes us who we are, so we attach to them. And because it's our life, we want to it to be 'perfect', right?

The truth is, whether it's in business or life, looking our disappointments and perceived failures in the eye, then having the courage and resilience to get back on our horse, surrender to the process of fumbling through to find our way, and finding our power again when we feel we've lost it, takes an inner strength. And sometimes, that strength seems hard to come by. But truthfully, it is always in you, and you can always call upon it. One way we can do this is by being really clear about what we have become too attached to, and finding a new way to flow with our life.

Liberate your expectations affirmation

I give myself permission to let go of my own timing, and to trust the bigger plan and the timing of my life. I am open to creating and receiving my dreams, or something better.

chapter 4

BE PROUD

Scared is what you're feeling.
Brave is what you're doing.

EMMA DONOGHUE, *ROOM*

Throughout the months after my perceived failure, I heard a lot from my inner critic and perfectionist. Thoughts like:

— *I can't believe you didn't do better.*
— *I can't believe this happened.*
— *Why didn't you see this train wreck before it hit?*
— *Why aren't you more successful by now? If you were, this wouldn't have happened.*
— *Why didn't you fix it sooner?*
— *What's wrong with you?*

My inner perfectionist wasn't happy, but a deeper part of myself, my true inner self was saying: 'Um, can you relax? I did the best I could do. I used what I had, and I started where I was. This was a huge learning experience. I did my best, and that is good enough.'

I was so focused on berating myself that I was, in fact, failing to see how much good work I'd done too.

Your best **is** good enough. Good enough is good enough. You might be thinking you failed because you did something wrong, or because you set expectations that were unattainable. But what if you were simply proud of how brave you had been, of how brave you **are** being?

I know we're all taught to 'reach for the stars' and, of course, that's wonderful. But you can reach for the stars while still believing that good enough is great too, and that being brave in trying is as important as succeeding.

— Be objective —

You don't need to be so 'all or nothing'. What is 'all' anyway? Do you really want nothing if you can't have it all? Of course not. Nothing is a void, but 'not having it all' still means you have so much.

To be objective means to step back, get some perspective and decide to rise above the noise of your inner perfectionist, who says you didn't do enough. If you did your best, and if you did it with an open heart and mind, that is good enough. That is enough.

If you approached the situation with an earnest wholeheartedness and with a devotion to do your best, that is enough. Being hard on yourself isn't the point. How much more brilliant to celebrate the fact that you tried at all?

— A text from my mum —

One day when I was being particularly hard on myself, I messaged my mum (as you do) and I received this reply from her: *Be proud of how brave you have been, taking a risk and following your dreams.* That message was a like a life raft, and I clung to it. I wrote it on a post-it and stuck it on my computer, where it stayed for many, many months.

But that reminder doesn't have to come from someone else; you can be the one who's proud of yourself. You can be the one who knows you were brave.

Be proud affirmation

I am proud of how brave I have been. I am proud of how brave I am being. I am doing my best, and I know that is enough.

---

chapter 5

THE BEST THINGS

The best things in life aren't always the expected things. In fact, the best things in life (free or not) are often the things we didn't plan, anticipate or expect, and that's why we open up to experience them so fully and magically.

I recently went to a beautiful yin yoga and sound healing workshop and I brought my hubby, Nic, along. As we stood outside the door to the event, several of our friends arrived too. None of us had realised we'd all booked the same event, and it was such a lovely surprise. The evening was so beautiful and was the perfect setting for a shift I needed to experience (which I'll tell you more about later in the book).

Afterwards, Nic and I had planned to go to a little wine bar nearby, so we invited all of our friends to join us. We sat outside under heaters in the chilly June air on this beautiful Saturday night, with blankets on our laps, laughter bubbling up through our throats, olives on our table, shiraz in our glasses and friends by our sides (joking about how it was so good that we'd just cleared our kidney and liver channels before having a glass of wine!).

It was one of those nights that you couldn't have planned, and it was perfect. And you know what I found so ironic? I've always wanted to sit at this particular wine bar on a Saturday night with friends but, for whatever reason, it had never eventuated. Either the bar had been too busy, or we'd run out of time to go before dinner, or for some other reason.

But on this night—this night where I had no expectations—I was incredibly, wonderfully, pleasantly surprised. And I took that feeling in, and let it wash through me, as a gentle reminder that **not** planning can feel as good as planning until the cows come home.

— Relaxing your expectations —

Let's put your expectations into perspective, shall we? When do you think they began?

Did you used to rock up to kindergarten and say to yourself: 'Okay, so today I think Tommy should play with me, but if we don't get the red truck from Billy first, I'm going to throw a tantrum. Annabelle better be sitting near me during snack time, because we have to discuss next week's puppet show. And honestly, if nap time isn't at 2pm on the dot, the day just won't be worth it, and I'm out.'

No. No, you didn't say that to yourself. You probably arrived at kindy and just excitedly leapt on the first friend you saw, played in the sandpit with whoever was in there, focused on the present moment and let snack time and nap time just come to you. (#KindyLyfe) How much more relaxed does this second scenario sound? And not just because it includes your three-year-old self, or snack time and nap time (we can have those things in our adult life too, you know).

The second scenario sounds more relaxed because it is more relaxed. It's where we are flowing, going, moving and letting life lead us. It's not about taking a back seat, playing the victim or feeling bitter or resentful when things don't go your way. It's about relinquishing control over the outcomes, because while we can own the outcome, we don't own the power to control it. (And really, we wouldn't want to anyway.)

How many times in your life have you had your heart set on something (or tried to control something), only to have the outcome turn out even better than you initially imagined?

Every time you try to control the outcome, you increase your expectations about how you want it to turn out. I understand this completely because not only have I felt this, and put myself through it time and time again, but because I see my clients going through it too. We like to know the answers, the ending and the completeness of our story. Sometimes we want to know how it ends before it's even begun. Through this fear and forcing, we create tension and tightness where none needs to exist. (Or at least, a lot less needs to exist.)

— Why are you rushing? —

When I think of having expectations, they always seem so time-heavy. Time seems to slow down, while I'm trying to speed it up. It sometimes feels as though if we don't grip harder on what we want, if we don't control and measure and dictate, then the ending won't matter because it won't be good enough.

Feeling comfortable to trust and surrender can be better understood if you think about baking a cake. Imagine if you invited friends over for your famous chocolate cake. You go to the grocery store and buy all the ingredients. Can you show your friends your cake yet? Well, no—you haven't made it yet. So you start baking, and you mix the batter. You want to whip the bowl around and show your friends because you're so excited about this cake! Except, of course, the cake isn't a cake yet. It's still batter.

So you put it in the oven. As soon as it's out you want to ice it because ... cake! But no, the cake is too hot. If you iced it now, it would melt everywhere and become a hot mess.

You can't show your friends until the time is right—until the ingredients have been purchased, the batter has been mixed, the cake has been baked, cooled and iced. Then you can show your friends. If you show them too soon, for your own excitement and pleasure, they won't get to witness or taste the magic that is your cake. They might just see that hot mess, with you running circles around them, apologising and saying it doesn't usually turn out that way.

You have to wait, just a little. (Without letting it feel like waiting.) You have to be patient. You have to take one step, and then the next becomes clear. One step ... then the next.

— Releasing your non-existent expectations —

Think back to your last 'disappointment.' I write it like that because often our disappointments are just lessons disguised in fear, shame or regret. I want you to really feel into it. Sit with the feelings and the sensations; the guilt, the grief, the regret. Let yourself feel it all. So often we bury those emotions and feelings, burrowing them into the earth of our despair and never simply letting them stay at the surface where they're actually so much easier to clear.

Sometimes expectations also camouflage themselves as wishes, intentions or just plain 'good luck.' We think that if we really want something to happen, it'll just happen because we deserve it, or because we've worked hard for it, or because we're entitled to it. Sometimes we think we'll be the recipient of our dreams and desires, just because.

There's nothing inherently wrong with this—but it can stunt our growth. That's because we may take less action, with less true intentions, because we think we'll get what we want anyway.

— Let it be a little bit messy —

I go to art classes for a few weeks every year, with a teacher I've been learning from since my high school days. I found myself back at art during this period of feeling a little lost, because I wanted to remind myself that I could make something beautiful, and be proud of it. I wanted to create with no expectations. (I also just wanted to take the pressure off myself and do something for the pure joy, fun and bliss of it!)

I started with two oil paintings on canvas, one of pears and one of lemons. I painted the lemons all shades of blue—cobalt and cerulean, with highlights of turquoise and white—inspired by a painting I saw and loved. The pears are raw umber, burnt umber, yellow ochre and raw sienna, with splashes of deep crimson. I love these painintgs, and they're still hanging up in our home to this day.

A few of the women in the art class loved these paintings of mine too. They could understand what they were; they could compare them with other paintings of pears and lemons and understand their context; they could see how they could make something like this too. They also loved that the lemons were blue, because why not?

Then I moved on to painting an abstract, using acrylic on canvas. I'd found a few images of abstract paintings on Pinterest, printed them out and intended to use elements of each painting as inspiration for my own.

I squeezed some paint onto my palette, put paintbrush to canvas and just flowed with what came through. All of a sudden, the women around me were saying things like: 'I can't paint abstract paintings; I just never know where to start or end; I never know if it's right' and 'But how do you know what you're doing? How do you know when it's finished?'

But I didn't need to know where I was going, or where to start or end. I just painted. Lashings of turquoise and aqua, blue and magenta, crimson and yellow. I loved painting this abstract even more than my pears and lemons, for exactly that reason—I could start and finish anywhere and it was all right, because I was defining what 'beautiful' and 'successful' looked like, on my own terms. No-one could say I was doing it incorrectly, because I was painting whatever I wanted to paint, whatever felt good, and putting colour and texture wherever I felt called to. I loved it.

And yes, that abstract painting is still hanging in our home as well.

It reminded me (and still reminds me, each time I look at it) that I can create something beautiful and, more importantly, that I can let go of expectations, define my own version of 'success' and love the outcome even more because of it.

Abstract paintings look beautiful because they're a little bit messy sometimes, because you can't see the beginning, the middle or the end. Because there is no beginning, middle or end. There is just beauty in all of it. And that's what your journey, your process, your initiation into surrendering, letting go, and stepping up again is all about too.

— **Managing expectations** —

Like the winds of change, expectations can come from anywhere, and hit us hard when we're least expecting it. How do we 'manage' expectations?

Well, the answer is … without managing them at all. We meet them where they're at, we show up with a full, open heart and a desire to show ourselves in the best way possible, and we say to our expectations, big or small: 'I see you. And I don't need you.'

Here are some questions to help you get clear on your expectations:

— What's the next thing you're hoping (or expecting!) will happen in your life? (This could be big or small, and related to any area of your life.)
— How are you hoping this will play out for you?
— How would you feel if your expectations did come true?
— What would you do next?
— How would you feel if your expectations didn't come true? (Think of all the pros and cons of the next best-case scenario, but also the 'less than best' case.)

— What would you do then? What would you have learnt and gained from this experience?

— No matter the outcome, would you still be okay as a person? (Hint: the answer is 'yes.')

I want you to give yourself permission to feel it all, so that you don't hide your emotions, fears, regrets or grief in your skin, tissues, organs, body, or any element of your mental, emotional and spiritual self.

And don't worry because, even if you do, this book will provide you with the tools, exercises and, most importantly, the awareness and permission to clear it all out.

The best things affirmation

I allow myself to stay open to experience magic, synchronicity and flow in my life. I know this is possible for me. I now open to new and wonderful experiences, intentions and ideas, and am committed to experiencing them fully and with an open heart, a clear mind and balanced energy.

WHEN YOU GET CLEAR ON YOUR
EXPECTATIONS AND RELEASE THEM,
YOU GET TO KEEP YOUR OPTIONS OPEN.

#itsallgoodbook

chapter 6

WE ARE THE MASTERS

What the caterpillar calls the end,
the master calls a butterfly.

RICHARD BACH

Remember playing the game *Duck Duck Goose* when you were little? You would sit in a circle at kindergarten, and someone would run around the outside perimeter shouting 'Duck! Duck! Duck!' and then randomly, 'Goose!' If you were tapped as the goose, you had to jump up and take your friend's place, running around the circle. But you never knew when 'goose' was coming, and that was the exciting part. That was what the game was about.

Imagine if it was all planned ahead, so no-one got upset, surprised or excited. Imagine if you knew what day of the week in every term you'd be tapped in as the goose. How boring. The game would lose all meaning, all excitement and all appeal. In fact, you probably wouldn't even want to play the game at all.

As much as we think we like knowing what's coming up next, the unknown can be such an adventure when we're open to it. In the opening chapter of *The Surrender Experiment*, Michael A. Singer writes: *Life rarely unfolds exactly as we want it to. And if we stop to think about it, that makes perfect sense.*

— We have free will —

My sister got married recently and at a pre-wedding event the rabbi asked us this question: 'If we had the choice to see our future, would we want to?'

Most people would be tempted to reply 'yes' straightaway. But what the rabbi explained was so beautiful. He said that no, we wouldn't, because then you would act from what you know will happen and it can create a self-fulfilling prophecy. In knowing our future, we would forget the most important thing: that we have free will. Nothing is set in stone. And not knowing our future means we have all the possibilities still before us.

Not knowing our future helps us to build a better life today. It's open and expansive. It's freeing.

It's so much more powerful to live from a space of trust, rather than tiresomely forcing and controlling an outcome, trying to know with certainty something that you can't know. If you knew your future, how would you act today? Maybe you'd try harder, or maybe you'd not try at all. Instead, be open to staying in trust, flowing with whatever comes your way, and acting in integrity and alignment with who you are.

— Stay open —

When you get clear on your expectations and release them, you get to keep your options open. So go on, open yourself up to some new adventures and be all in. Be the light in your life and be open to beautiful new possibilities and experiences. Don't try to control absolutely everything in your life. Let yourself be pleasantly surprised. It doesn't have to be scary and controlling; it can be light and fun.

What I know for sure is this: we may never have all our ducks in a row. And sometimes, we may feel like an absolute goose. But this doesn't need to stop us from taking steps towards what we want to align ourselves to with an open heart and mind.

What I want you to remember is that you don't need the false security of perfectionism and procrastination, of force and willpower, of twisting events and circumstances into something that 'fits' to be healthy, happy, and purposeful.

— Getting clear —

As I write this in real time, I'm only several months past the publication date of my first book, *You Are Enough*. Because of all of my past experiences with setting the world's highest expectations, I had a very clear intention before my first book launched: I wanted to go into the experience with absolutely no expectations.

This was a new way of approaching things for me. Going into my book launch period feeling clear, light and easy about myself, meant that if something wonderful happened, I could be pleasantly surprised. If something less than best happened, I could take action from a calm space. And if nothing happened, I wouldn't be reactive or disappointed (and then, in turn, I could take action from a calm space to invite in some flow).

As it turned out, many absolutely wonderful things happened (with a few exciting things happening even before the official publication date!). So I truly saw—perhaps for the first time in a very long time—how beautiful and beneficial it is to be clear of expectations, so we can be open to pure possibility.

It truly is possible to be present in your life, without always looking forward to your next expectation and wondering how and when it'll show up for you, and whether it'll be as perfect as you'd like it to be.

Instead of setting unyielding targets, you can set intentions that don't weigh you down with expectation and disillusionment. You can do this by being open to the possibilities of the unknown, without being scared of the unknown. You can do this by saying to yourself: 'This is something that would feel really good to me, but I'm also open to it looking different, because I trust that's what's right for me.'

You can do this by trusting in yourself, and in a higher power, and by deeply believing that you don't need all the pieces of your puzzle now, to start laying down some foundations for your dreams.

— Before you can let go —

Before you can let go of your past disappointments, you must accept where you are, where your dreams are, and make a commitment to yourself to find that middle ground again.

The middle ground is where you are now, and your dreams are yet to be realised, but you're happy with where you are. Embodying this doesn't take away from your goals to improve, craft, hone, succeed and do incredible things. But it means you must ground yourself in the now, in this moment, where things maybe didn't turn out how you expected them to, where the pieces aren't all fitting together just yet, but you can see there's still space for beauty.

This moment, now, is perfectly and wonderfully okay. And when you are here, you are further away from your regret and disappointments, because those moments live in the past and you, my dear, are at this moment, here, now.

— Your best days —

One of my favourite sayings (although I can't remember where I heard it) is: *Our best days are still in front of us.* That's the energy I like to embody when thinking about my future. How does that feel to you?

When you start to let go of your disappointments, trust you'll keep the lessons that you've learnt. And always add a sweet side dish of trust to your visions and dreams. Trust that your intentions will manifest in the right time and in the right form for you. Trust that you're on the right path. (Even when you **really** don't believe it.)

Trust that the lessons you're learning are simply that— lessons. When you start to surrender to where you are and trust in the bigger plan, you'll believe that you're not being punished or berated. You'll know—without a doubt—that there's nothing inherently wrong with you at all, in any way, shape or form. You're human, learning human lessons, and feeling human pain (as well as joy, beauty and bliss).

And trust that at the end of all of this, everything will be okay.

Your best days affirmation

I allow myself to dream and set goals, and also to be open to something even better flowing to me. I trust that my intentions will manifest in the right time and in the right form for me. I trust that I'm on the right path.

YOUR FAILURE IS NOT THE

END OF YOUR WORLD.

———

#itsallgoodbook

chapter 7

YOUR PERCEPTION
IS EVERYTHING

———

*It takes guts and humility to change
your mind. Fortunately, you have the
freedom and the courage to do so.*

SETH GODIN

nderstanding your perception of your situation—what
is real and true, and not what's based on your ego's
chitchat—is a crucial element of surrendering, flowing and
trusting. Without understanding and acceptance, we can stay
stuck. It's important to be able to recognise if we're stuck at
this stage of the process and how to move on from it.

Have you ever thought that accepting something means
you cannot change it? I used to feel that too, but now I
see that **acceptance is what makes something changeable**.
When you can accept, you can change. On the other hand,
when you fight, you cannot flow.

Acceptance is your gateway to changing your perception, and your perception is your gateway into surrendering to where you are.

— Your perception is everything, and you can change it whenever you want —

There are a few ways we can shift our perception. You know how if you're in a bad mood and a friend says, 'Oh just lighten up! You'll be fine, get over it,' that usually doesn't help the situation? It's because, even if it's coming from a tender place, someone else is trying to force your hand into shifting your energy.

Now imagine giving yourself permission to change your mind, to see things differently, to look at your situation from another angle so as to see it in a new light, with a new perspective.

Ah, what freedom that would invite in! Freedom to think about yourself and your situation differently. Freedom to accept the outcome and then still show up as your best self, even if things didn't go to plan. Freedom to let yourself feel whatever comes up for you—anger, rage, disappointment, fear, sadness—knowing that you have the courage to witness and move through those emotions too.

Sometimes we just have to feel what we're feeling, instead of bulldozing through it. I always say to my clients, 'You don't judge yourself for feeling happy, so why do you judge yourself for feeling sad?' Be in it ... so you can let it pass. See it, feel it, then step aside and let it wash away, or step through it and let it dissolve. But don't try to stand so vehemently in its way that it ends up crushing you.

Take the judgement out, and your perception will be cleaner, clearer and lighter. You'll be able to see that your situation, your pain is just an experience you're going through, and that there's nothing wrong with you. You're just feeling the breadth of emotions that comes with being human and this is a good thing.

— Stay hopeful —

There's a good reason why hope is thought of as one of the most powerful emotions: once we lose hope, we lose faith, we feel as though we've lost our strength, and we lose the ability to empower ourselves.

Once we lose hope, we let go because of apathy and resentment, which is not the same as letting go and surrendering to where we are. If you feel as though you can't go on, be compassionate to yourself, stay hopeful, and stay in touch with your needs and desires, because things can change for the better in less than a moment.

— Pick yourself up (you can do it) —

Sometimes when you go through a disappointment, it feels as if you are alone in carrying the burden of your 'shoulds,' your expectations and your defeatism. It can sometimes feel hard to explain to someone else just how much you're hurting, especially if your dream felt so big and so personal, that you never truly expressed it outside of yourself.

When this happens, it's normal and natural to want to retreat. Sometimes this is to hide, sometimes this is to process and integrate, and sometimes it's an ambiguous combination that needs our gentleness and softness to smooth it over.

Sometimes we even want to fight the disappointment, thinking it through over and over again, running over every other possibility in our minds until we feel trapped and frantic.

Disappointments can be confusing and sometimes even confronting. They ask us to look our desires and defeat in the eye. They ask us questions we don't think we could bear to answer: 'What will you do now? How will you get over this and get through it? And then what?'

No matter how you feel when you think you've fallen short, please don't think it's just all about you; you aren't being punished, you're not a bad person, and no, you didn't 'deserve' this. Those thoughts, although very common, are not truly helpful, are they? They keep us stuck in a spiral of despair, when the truth is we must create our own positive and hopeful staircase, to help take us back up to the heights of our potential.

The next time you feel disappointed—big or small, light as a feather or substantially crushing—let it in, all of it. Feel the breadth and depth of your emotions: hurt, anger, rage, sadness, pain, fear, regret. Don't tell yourself what you 'should' do or feel. Let yourself feel what you're actually feeling, with no judgement and no brushing it away.

Then allow yourself to process, to integrate, to reflect, to release and to breathe a sigh of relief. It can be over. The pain can shift. The lesson can stay. And as the saying goes: *Try, try again.*

— It is what it is … or is it? —

My whole body tenses when people shrug their shoulders and say things like: 'It is what it is.' Yes, it is what it is …

but when said with such nonchalance this feels like such a powerless statement. It has the essence of surrender, but it's not the full flavour.

The way to begin the process of accepting a situation or disappointment for what it is—instead of for what we were attached to it being—is to do so while staying in our power, by owning our decisions and actions, and letting ourselves change and shift our perception.

— There are other ways to get what we want —

Creating expectations is a perception, and we can change our perceptions.

If we really align ourselves to the best possible outcome, do we automatically get what we want, when we want it, and exactly how we imagined it? No. Yes. Maybe. I can't really answer that question, because the answer will never be the same.

In *You Are Enough*, the message is about helping you believe that you are indeed worthy; that you can believe in yourself and trust yourself. Now we take that concept a step further. If you trust yourself, it's easier to trust in the universe, right? Right. That's where I'd like you to go; to trust that while you can't control the outcomes, you can trust yourself, your intuition, your decisions, and your path in life. You can show up as your very best self in your life (crystal ball not included).

Getting through challenges and coming out stronger on the other side isn't about fighting our way through it; it's about softening some parts of ourselves, and strengthening others. It's about acknowledging our 'perceived' failures and trusting that we can stand up again, during them and after them. It's about knowing that everything we go through is worth it, and that we can accept our journeys, no matter where we are.

— Fearful (and tired) of goal setting —

When I was at my low point, I became terrified of goal setting. I felt like no matter what goals I set for myself, no matter how much action I was taking, they weren't coming to fruition in the way I wanted them to. I was scared to set new goals, because I thought I'd missed some crucial element in my previous experience. I worried that until I'd worked out what went wrong, everything I attempted would be a failure from now on.

It took me a long, long time to work through this because, while I really do like achieving my goals, I was terrified of failing again. I felt like I couldn't put myself through the same thing again. Of course, I also knew I was being a tiny bit dramatic, and that I was making things much worse in my head. What I had to do was acknowledge that just because I was setting goals, that didn't mean I had to hit every one. From then on, whenever I set a new goal or intention in my life, I started to give myself more breathing room, more flow.

I began to remind myself that, even if I failed again, I was still worthy and still on the right track. Whenever I 'failed,' that was a lesson in and of itself. Or perhaps not a lesson at all—a missed goal is just one thread in the tapestry of your entire life.

Not surprisingly, if there was to be a lesson contained within the experience of my failure, that lesson was almost the same, time and time again. I was being taught that if I wasn't in my flow, and completely open to whatever needed to happen for my highest good (even if I didn't agree with it), then I would be left feeling confused or upset about the outcome.

This realisation marked a turning point for me. This wasn't about goal setting, or even about intention setting. This was about my inner settings. This was about crafting my inner world to be the truthful container for what I wanted to draw into my outer world.

— Set them anyway —

During this period where I was afraid to set new goals and dreams again, I spoke to a friend who told me that she often didn't reach her goals, but that never stopped her from setting them and working towards them anyway.

I absolutely loved hearing her say this. For such a long time, I had thought that setting a goal meant I had to achieve it; and if I didn't achieve it, I had failed. Talking to my friend and hearing her perception of goal setting completely shifted mine.

What about if you set goals and, of course, did your best to achieve them, but also congratulated yourself for simply trying, for showing up, even if the goals didn't turn out how you wanted them to?

— What would happen if your goals didn't happen? —

If your goals don't become reality, you will still be okay. You might be disappointed and the lesson might sting, but you'll

be okay. You'll get through it, you'll find another way, or …
you'll let it go entirely.

We forget this sometimes, in times of strife and need
and crazy desire for something bigger and better. We forget
that if this 'thing' we wanted didn't eventuate, we would
actually still be okay. You know why we forget sometimes?
We forget because our fear and insecurity get the better of
us. Our fear tells us that we're doing the wrong thing, that
we're on the wrong path, and that we'll never be okay again.
Our insecurities tell us that we're missing out, that we've
ruined everything, and that we're now unlovable and we'll
be unsuccessful forever. What drama!

Let's break this plot down, because I have felt that fear
and there were times when I let it drown me. But that didn't
help me. What did? Realising that, in truth, my fear was not
my oracle and that, indeed, everything was going to be okay.

A new perspective affirmation

*I give myself permission to let go of the outcome, and
to still show up as my best self. I allow myself to see a
new perspective, to help me move towards my dreams
and goals (or something better) with ease and flow.*

OUR FAILURE CREATES OUR LIGHT.

#itsallgoodbook

chapter 8

YOUR FAILURE CAN BE YOUR PROGRESSION

Heroes often fail.

GORDON LIGHTFOOT, *IF YOU COULD READ MY MIND*

Think back to all your favourite fairytales. Cinderella lost her (probably very expensive and definitely designer) glass shoe. Belle almost killed her Beast. We all fail sometimes (even heroes). It's human nature.

— Growing pains —

When I think of all the lessons I learnt through my failure, I can see that I actually accelerated my growth on so many levels. The pain wasn't so much in the lessons I learnt, but in the speed I learnt them. Talk about growing pains!

Let's go through some of the positive aspects of failure now. Hopefully, you'll be able to attribute some of your own lessons to this list and see how your perceived failure was a catalyst for your own beautiful growth too.

— Failure makes us stronger —

Well this one's obvious, although sometimes a bit painful. You will always learn something from being challenged, and you'll be so much stronger because of it.

Our failure creates our light. As the late Leonard Cohen so famously sang: *There's a crack in everything. That's how the light gets in.* (Ah, I get goosebumps as I type that.)

— Failure helps us declutter —

When we decide to take our lessons and use them to do better next time, we also let go of the things we no longer need. This might mean decluttering old mindsets and limiting beliefs, perceived rules you've placed upon yourself or had placed on you by others, stuff you no longer need (physical, mental, emotional or spiritual), and even letting go old relationships.

Sometimes this happens on your terms, and sometimes part of the pain is because of other people's choices. Either way, there's a feeling of starting anew and it's one you can grab with both hands and dive right into.

— Failure helps us see clearly —

Similarly to gaining mental strength and decluttering, failure helps us to get clarity on what's important to us. Our new goals become crystal clear—even if that's after a brief period of intense confusion and overwhelm, even if feels like our failure has slowed us down or sent us off track. Much of the energetic clearing of the energy of failure lies in your ability to see the bigger picture, and your ability to invite in clarity. This is how you grow.

— Failure helps us connect —

Our struggles don't separate us, they connect us. If you've gone through a hard time, someone else has felt that too. Don't let your ego or your inner critic trick you into thinking that you're the only person this has ever happened to. Don't carry all that pain on your shoulders. We're all doing this thing called life together. Reach out if you need help. There is someone waiting to connect with you, help you, support you and lift you up.

— Failure can create momentum —

Sometimes we think failure has stalled us. But what if your failure was your propulsion, and now you have an even clearer idea of where you're going, why you want to go there and how you'll get there?

What if your failure gave you the fuel to fight for your dreams again? What if your focus has increased, and your mind is stronger, and your spirit is guiding you to a new level?

Where has your failure taken you?

— Failure helps us tune into gratitude —

When we think we've failed, or when things aren't going the way we want them to, it's sometimes easy to get stuck in a swirling cesspool of negativity, doubt, confusion and fear. This doesn't mean that other elements of our life aren't feeling good to us; it's just that we're focusing on what's not working, not happening, and not flowing to us.

What's sometimes so ironic is that this duality exists: where one area of our lives can feel and be so flowing and beautiful, and another part feels stuck and stagnant.

Why not tune into what is working for you right now? What is feeling good in your life? Where can you see and feel momentum and flow? Honour this, and invest some energy and attention into being grateful for the good in your life.

— To be (stuck), or not to be (stuck) —

When we feel stuck, we often look to the 'one' thing that can help us get unstuck. We want a quick fix out of our discomfort, a way out that is instant and easy, something to do that'll help shift our energy and get us feeling right back into ourselves. Sometimes we look to healthy options, sometimes to options that are less than healthy (whatever your own vice may be). Sometimes we numb the pain, wondering if it'll ever disappear, but mostly we just want the pain to dissolve, no matter what it takes.

Many times though, shifting our stuckness isn't just about action—it's about being, and being in it. Shifting our energy and any surrounding stuckness is about our mindset and attitude, and not merely just about our to-do lists and quick fixes. It can so often be about not trying to change the situation, but to be okay about being in it.

This can sometimes make us feel even more stuck. I know, I know. We like to take action! And do stuff! And be proactive! And make change happen! But honestly, really and truly, sometimes you simply have to feel the spectrum of your feelings. You have to get down and dirty with how you're feeling and, no matter what you find there, whisper to them (or shout or scream or write poetry) and say 'I see you! I'm not scared to feel you, to see you, to hold you and then to release you. I see you. I trust you'll pass. But for now, I am still okay.'

I've been there too; we all have. I was there for many months once. While taking aligned and inspired action helped, sometimes there wasn't much about the outcome that felt aligned or inspired. Sometimes it felt like I was just going around and around in circles, fighting my way out of a maze that never wanted to let me go. It was frustrating and overwhelming at times.

There was a part of me that knew this wouldn't last, but there was also fear: 'What if this is your new forever? What if you'll never truly get out of this, now that you've seen a darker side?'

That was my ego speaking. That was fear, pain, confusion, overwhelm, panic and a perceived sense of powerlessness trying to consume me. Sometimes it won. Mostly I fought back in my own way. As often as I could, I tried to remind myself to do this not by controlling (oh, but how I wanted to control!) but instead, by doing my very best to **be** there. To feel it. To not wallow, to not sink, to not disappear in my 'problems', but to just acknowledge them, to witness them, to see them with a more distant approach, so as to not start to see my world through the lens of bitterness and lack.

In hindsight, we see so clearly. And I can see that one of the ties that kept my perception bound to this sense of failure was that I wasn't forgiving myself. Sure, I was doing forgiveness work, but not enough—not fully, not completely.

I'm not writing this book with the intention that you start believing we never have to go through uncomfortable moments in our lives. It's because I want you to believe that you can thrive despite those uncomfortable moments (and if not always thrive, know you can survive them!). And that sometimes we truly do have to be in those moments, feel them completely and surrender to them, in order for them to pass—unpleasant as it may be.

— Failure as progression —

Answer these questions to help get some clarity on your failures and challenges:

— What has my failure or challenge taught me?

— What has surprised me about this experience?

— What good has come of this experience?

— What will I do with this information and wisdom moving forward?

So, let yourself fail. Fail wonderfully. Fail miserably. Just let yourself fail. It's all good, you'll be okay, and everything will be okay. Your failure is not the end of your world.

Failure as progression affirmation

I allow myself to acknowledge and absorb the lessons from my failures. I know I am strong enough to move forward with wisdom, compassion and ease.

chapter 9

THE FEAR OF IT

---

*I*f we weren't so scared of our failures, we would barely notice them. If we didn't put so much pressure on ourselves to reach our goals with rigidity and perfectionism, on our own timeline, then disappointments would feel as light as feathers, instead of sometimes weighing us down like bricks.

When we do finally face our fear of failure, we can see the beauty of ourselves in our fear's reflection. Our fear stops having power over us, because our strength takes priority.

I know this might not happen all the time (sometimes when we go through a difficult situation, we can become more fearful of old patterns repeating in the future) but I invite you now to think of a failure or disappointment that you can look back on and say to yourself: 'Well it happened, but I'm still here. And I'm not scared of that happening again, because I already know I can get through it.'

I can think of an example from my own life. My high school boyfriend had a dog that hated me. I love dogs, I've grown up with them, and I've never met a dog who I didn't get along with, except this one. Initially, I tried to make friends with him, but when that failed miserably, I tried to never be alone with that dog as he would growl at me, and I felt uncomfortable around him.

One day I was sitting on the couch by myself and the dog jumped up next to me. As soon as I locked eyes on his, I knew he was about to bite me. I ducked my head down to try and seem less threatening, but I could tell there was no escape. I was too scared to even call out to my boyfriend, in case the dog became frightened and bit me. I tried to get up very carefully, non-threateningly, but to no avail. The dog lunged at my face and I lifted my arm up to protect myself. His bite—on the fleshy bit on the back of my arm—left a huge, colourful bruise for days.

But despite this experience, I didn't become more scared of him—this very tiny dog with a very big bite. I became less scared of him. I surrendered to the fact that he didn't like me, or that he felt threatened by me; I surrendered to the fact that he had a very painful bite, and I stayed even further away from him. Instead of trying to become his friend as I had in the past, I just let it all go.

This might seem like an insignificant example, but again, the lesson is universal: sometimes we become aware that things aren't going our way, and yet we simultaneously know that the only way is through it, even though the shit is about to hit the fan. Sometimes, the mere fact that you survived is enough to propel you forwards with strength and resilience, more than you knew you had.

If you can look your fear in the face, you can also shift your perspective and see your strength and resilience. Same mirror, different angle.

Releasing fear affirmation

It's safe for me to look my fear in the eyes. I know I am strong and resilient. I know I can manage whatever is in front of me beautifully, and with ease, grace and honour.

Now, take a deep, cleansing, calming breath in. In the next chapter, we're moving on and letting go.

chapter 10

KEEP THE GOLDEN NUGGET

These mountains that you are carrying,
you were only supposed to climb.

NAJWA ZEBIAN

While letting go is one of the first steps in surrendering, it can feel so hard sometimes. It's time to put a healing balm on the pain of holding on, if you're finding it hard to let go.

In this chapter, I'll invite you to look at, acknowledge and then let go of some of the feelings of grief, guilt, regret and pain that we can so often (and so easily) feel when we think we've failed.

We can suppress our emotions for so many reasons, and a step further than that is suppressing our stories. We try to brush them over for fear of really looking at them.

Another way we suppress our stories is—ironically—by overconsuming them. We look at them so much that we push them further and further down into the creases of who we are. Then we start to believe that **what** happened to us is **who** we are. But this is not a supportive practice. This keeps us stuck in the negative energy of the stories we've told ourselves about the event, the circumstance, the failure.

Overconsuming a failure becomes more and more bitter, until it becomes harder and harder to taste anything else—to taste the sweetness of setting new intentions, of working towards new goals, and of receiving what we desire, or (yep, you guessed it) something better.

For us to let go of the idea or story that we've failed, we need to truly let go of the pain in the lesson, forgive ourselves, and keep the gem, the jewel of the old story. We really can let go of our stories of perceived failure. If we don't let these stories go, we cannot surrender, we cannot move forward, and we cannot create something new, exciting and wonderful for ourselves.

One way to ensure you're ready to let go fully is to get clear on everything you think you've done wrong or badly, so you can compassionately clear it. For me, one of the ways I could start to get clear on my story was through journaling. If I found myself in a slump, constantly rethinking all the things I was being hard on myself about, I'd have to move that energy out of myself in order to feel clearer. Writing it out was one of the simplest and best ways to do so.

You are not what happened to you. If you failed an exam, are you a failed exam? Obviously not. Does this mean you'll fail every exam you'll ever take? Um, no. If you spilt a litre of milk on the floor, are you a puddle of spilt milk? Does this mean you can never be trusted with milk again? No. If you step in dog poo in brand new shoes, can you never buy new shoes again? Don't be ridiculous. So stop defining yourself because of one replayed event in your mind.

You are what you absorbed and digested—and then what you let go—from the situation. You don't need to hold on to what happened to you so tightly. You don't need to define yourself in the eyes of a situation, a circumstance, an event. You don't need to overconsume the situation again and again and again. You don't need to download the video in your mind and replay it until the tape wears out, until you wear yourself thin with guilt, grief, shame and regret.

You need to let it go. You need to define your own story. This doesn't mean you forget what you've been through; it means you remember it, all the lessons and the pain and the joy and the expansion, and you choose to keep on keeping on anyway. You need to get clear on what you can take from the situation, what you can absorb and digest and, as importantly, what you can let go.

— Rewriting your story and letting go —

When I was in primary school, we went on an excursion to a country town which, back in ye olden days, was the hub of the Australian gold rushes in the nineteenth century. My school friends and I were taken down to a muddy river, given these flat sieve-like contraptions, and shown how to look for gold (that had obviously been planted there that morning by the excursion coordinators).

We had to dip our sieves into the river water, shaking them from side to side until all the water, mud and debris had fallen away. Hopefully, all that ended up in our sieves were little flecks of gold. Excellent!

We washed away the debris, and we kept the golden nugget. It's a beautiful way to think of learning lessons, right? So, think of this example when going through some of these upcoming tools. Think of clearing the mud, the dirt, the debris, and keeping the little nugget of golden wisdom that is all yours. Think about letting go of the hurt, and keeping the jewels of your story, of your pain.

— You have to look your story in the eyes —

Let's get your story straight, okay? This isn't through the eyes of others, this isn't your perception of how others perceive you. This is **your** story; what you're thinking, feeling, acting on or reacting to. This is where you get to scrap what's not working for you, edit the rough parts, polish what feels really good, and publish what lights you up.

Grab a fresh sheet of paper and segment it into four squares. At the top of the first square, write the word 'Scrap.' At the top of the second square, write the word 'Edit' and so on with 'Polish' and 'Publish,' so each segment has a different heading.

— In the Scrap section —

Scribble, scrawl and write down everything from a recent situation (or just in general) that truly isn't working for you. This could be a negative thought pattern, a perception you have that isn't serving you, regrets over things you could have, should have or would have said or done differently.

This is your **letting go** quadrant—this is where you write it out, to let it go. If you need more space than just one square, feel free to write pages and pages. If you want to then throw out the papers, or scrawl through them or draw over them or burn them, you can. You can 'scrap' this scrap section in any way that feels good to you. Sometimes, this means putting an element of it aside to tweak and edit later.

But be mindful: what do you feel you need to hold onto for your highest good; and what just feels scary to let go of? Only you will know. The purpose of scrapping is to look it in the eye and say: 'Hey, is this working? Because if it's not really working for me anymore, I'm letting it go.' And then, let it go.

This is you writing down the old story in a way that feels good to you. This could be in dot points, a mind map or brainstorm, words or phrases that jump out at you, or a full script of what's been going on for you.

If you find you're telling yourself you don't know how to start, or how to journal, just say, 'Thanks for sharing' and get back to it. You can write down your story, and you can own it.

I want you to be as honest, frank and raw as you need to be. No-one is looking at this but you, so tell yourself the truth of your story. What feels like it worked? What feels like it didn't work? And if something didn't work, is it actually a failure?

— In the Edit section —

This section is about taking things that feel like they're mostly working, but you know you want to invest in or expand on in some way. You don't need to write down seventeen things; it can just be a couple of things that you want to work on over the next little while. As an example, it might be that you want to speak more kindly to yourself, or give yourself more time to rest and restore your energy. You may want to be more compassionate to others in your life, or you may simply want to eat more vegetables. There's no right or wrong. In fact, you may like to take elements of what you wrote down in the Scrap section and edit them. What would make them feel better, or work better for you?

This isn't about being hard on yourself, searching for perfectionism or looking backwards and chewing over old patterns again. This is about saying to yourself: 'Okay, now that I know what I know, what can I do differently next time?' How can you allow something that feels stuck, feel clean and clear? How can you feel into your flow, honouring and acknowledging how it feels in your body, so you can draw even more of it into your life?

— In the Polish section —

In the Polish section, you'll do some inner work. Is there anything you need to do for yourself, in order to move forward? What would make you feel stronger right now? Think of this as the glue that's sticking all your other sections together. Without self-love and self-care, none of the other sections will really fuse together anyway.

Compassion, then expansion, then growth.

— In the Publish section —

Now that you've done all this work, how are you showing up in the world? How do you want to show up in the world? Are you feeling clearer and calmer? More compassionate to yourself, more loving, forgiving and accepting?

In this section, write out some affirmations, some intentions or some gratitude statements. Get clear on what you've learnt from this situation through rewriting your story. Is this the story you want to live? Show yourself that you're clear on your intentions, your aims and your purpose. Then ... live them.

— **The letting go breathing ritual** —

You know when people say, 'Oh, take a deep breath and count to ten; you'll feel so much better!' Well, that never used to work for me ... until I did it in a new way.

This little ritual is for those moments you feel reactive, whether big or small:

— Inhale slowly to the count of five, using your intention to gather up all the energy in and around you that's leaving you feeling agitated, angry, annoyed, sad or anything else.

— Hold your breath at the top for a moment, to be sure you've felt the intensity of what you need to feel. Then on a slow exhale to the count of five, let it go, let it go, let it go.

— At the end of your exhale, pause for a moment before your next inhale; see how you are okay, even in the space between your breaths? Remember this.

— Repeat that process as often as you need to.

As a final, gentle reminder, let's go back to the quote by Najwa Zebian that opened this chapter:

These mountains that you are carrying, you were only supposed to climb.

What are you still carrying? Why are you still carrying it? Why don't you put it down, and climb it instead?

— Can you let go of too much? —

I'm clearly all for letting go and releasing what we don't need but there's one tiny catch. You don't need to let go of absolutely everything, absolutely all the time.

Without contradicting all my writing on forgiveness and letting go, let me explain: I've seen this before, where friends or clients think they continually need to let go, let go, let go and purge, purge, purge their spiritual inadequacies. I can see their suffering in this space, and I can see it doesn't feel good. If you feel tempted to fall into that trap, it's a reminder to come back to the truth that **you are already enough**. You don't need to let go of everything in order to be more.

Letting go is a process of helping you move on towards more light, but thinking you're never letting go of enough keeps you trapped in the dark—it's a form of self-doubt, and a lack of confidence. So please, let go of what you need, as you need to, and when you need to; but don't trick yourself into thinking you're not good enough unless you're purged of darkness.

You don't need to fill every waking hour with inner work, intense clearing and deep healing, in order to show up as your best self today. Don't put your life on hold until you're 'healed'—isn't that just perfectionism and procrastination in its prettiest dress?

We all have a shadow self, a part of us that is a little bit darker, that isn't always understood or seen, and this is okay. You don't need to get rid of it all; you still need something to balance the light. It all has its purpose, and your purpose is not perfectionism. So don't let yourself be fooled by the notion that you're not good enough if you haven't 'perfectly purged' yourself.

If you do find yourself in that space, I find that getting out of your head and into your body is one of the best remedies. A compassionate way to do this is through breath and movement, and more movement. Get back into your body by going to yoga, or a run, a long walk, a swim or a cycle. I find forward movement (like walking) can often be incredibly beneficial, because of the simple fact that I'm moving forwards. Bodywork like massage is also helpful here, even if it's you massaging your own body, just to get your senses back into your body and your focus out of your head.

Letting go affirmation

It is safe for me to let go of all I no longer need. I open up to guidance on how to best let go and move forward, and I do this with self-compassion, self-love and self-awareness.

---

chapter 11

A BONE TO PICK

---

*I*f you find yourself about to let go, but then holding back, let me ask you: 'Are you holding a grudge against yourself?'

I would sometimes find myself thinking:

> *I forgive myself, but I'll just rehash that failure one more time ...*
>
> *I forgive myself, but I'm now going to punish myself just a little bit for what I think I did wrong, so that I definitely don't do it again ...*

Or my favourite one:

> *I forgive myself, but only if I remind myself of all the things I did wrong and try to work out how I could redo them in the past, even though it's impossible to travel back in time to do things differently. But I'm going to try anyway, dammit!*

I can tell you, this isn't true forgiveness. It's conditional, it doesn't last, and it doesn't feel good. It's also exhausting and can take the place of the necessary inner healing work, sometimes for months on end. In precious hindsight, I can see I spent a long time holding a grudge against myself.

Do you know what I used to do sometimes? I would sit down with a notebook, make tea, light a candle then literally brainstorm ways I could have done things differently, with the same fervour as if I were brainstorming a new project. What a waste of energy! I tricked myself into thinking this was a beneficial process, that I was reflecting and letting go, but in reality I was punishing myself.

It's like when people rub their puppy's nose in its pee, as if to say: 'Look how terrible you are! Look at this terrible job you've done! What is wrong with you?'

Do you know about the 'new' way of puppy training? It's to ignore the 'accident' if your puppy pees in the wrong place, and to clean it up when they're not looking (so they don't see anger or irritation in your body language as you clean it up). Then you pointedly treat and reward your puppy when they pee in the right place.

In this way, they have no negative connotations with failure; all their energy is in their reward. So they continue to pee in the right place; no grudges are held, no punishments are made and everyone is happy.

— Fake forgiveness —

Holding a grudge against yourself is fake forgiveness, like when you find yourself saying to someone: 'I'm sorry you think I upset you, but ...' If you were really sorry and fully compassionate, you'd accept responsibility and truly apologise. So, now it's time to be compassionate and truly apologise to yourself.

In the next chapter, we move on to a healing and forgiveness tool. But to use it, you have to want to forgive yourself. Don't hold a grudge against yourself (or anyone else, in fact) for what you've done or where you've been, for what you did or didn't do, for the goals you think you missed, or the limits you don't think you pushed. That's in the past. You're here now, today, in this very moment. Be here.

Don't let your past define your present, your future or your potential. Drop your grudge against yourself like it's hot (even though it's not!). Now let's move on, shall we?

(That's probably the most tough-love-esque I'll get in this entire book, but I think we all needed to hear it, right?)

Real forgiveness affirmation

I give myself full and complete permission to deeply forgive myself, on every level and dimension. It is safe for me to do this, and I am completely ready, willing and able to forgive myself.

---

chapter 12

WE GROW BY LETTING GO

And if it feels like you're losing
control, let go. Just let go.

VAULTS, *MIDNIGHT RIVER*

orgiveness can feel really hard, I know. But it's so important to do, and something we truly need to embrace in order to let go and flow with life. In this chapter, we'll look at why we need to forgive in order to move on (even if this feels so hard to do), plus we'll go through a beautiful energetic tool that will help you move more easily through the process of forgiveness.

I think that forgiving ourselves can be even harder than forgiving others sometimes, because we hold ourselves to such high standards. The fact that you're reading this book means I can be pretty sure that in the past, or perhaps right this very moment, there is something—or many things—for which you think you cannot forgive yourself.

Sometimes these are very, very old things. Memories, feelings, perceptions from the past, from another time when we thought differently, acted differently, maybe didn't have the same self-awareness. Sometimes these things are very, very recent.

Maybe there's a thought pattern, making its way around and around, getting stuck on the exact moment you think you said the wrong thing, the precise second you think you should have jumped in with a witty remark, a thank you, a sorry or some other perfectly-crafted sentence that only came to you when you'd already walked away.

Forgiving yourself is one of the first few tentative steps you must make if you're to surrender, if you're to find your flow, if you're to stay in your flow, so that beautiful opportunities can come to you, and so that beautiful possibilities stay open to you.

Forgiveness leads to flow, and being in your flow is more powerful than any amount of begrudging could ever be. We do not grow by holding on. We grow by letting go.

We do not grow by begrudging ourselves for our past. We grow by acknowledging everything that has come before this present moment, embracing it all under the umbrella of who we are, and forgiving ourselves for what we think we should have done differently. If you could go back and change something, you wouldn't be the person you are right now.

It's like the butterfly effect—have you heard of that? In chaos theory, it's the idea that the flapping of a butterfly's wings in one country can cause a hurricane on the other side of the world. When used as a metaphor, it's the idea that one small change can cause huge effects. If we apply that here, it's the idea that if it were even possible to go back in time and change just one tiny thing in your world, your entire universe would look different in this present moment. And the truth of that is that not everything would necessarily be better, or perfect, or exactly as you'd planned it.

If the idea of letting go feels like you're losing control, go with it. You only feel like you're losing control because you're trying to hold on and control so much. So just let go. Let go.

Everything needs to be where it is right now, for you to be who you are right now. And who you are right now is enough.

— Forgiveness Movement as a healing tool —

I'm calling this a Forgiveness Movement instead of an activity (even though it totally is an activity) because what's the opposite of movement? Inertia, stasis, stuckness and lack of momentum. (A few things you're probably not wanting to create in your life.)

So this Forgiveness Movement is here to help you release stuckness and sadness, and shift into true movement and momentum. It's about burning down and releasing what you no longer need, to make space for new life, new energy, new thought patterns and new (expectation-free) possibilities.

It's not quite the phoenix rising from the fire (that'll come later in the book, and in your journey), but it's where you must start, in order to rise again.

Here are some things you might like to have nearby while we go through this activity. I can almost hear a sigh of relief from you: 'Ah, I can take action and get stuff together to forgive myself!' Yes, but the inner work is the important work, so even if you don't gather the tools listed below, you can still forgive yourself. (Ha, gotcha!)

Let's begin with the essential tools:

— A decluttered and quiet space to do this work, where you feel comfortable, safe to speak out loud to yourself, to cry if you need to, and to truly express yourself without fear or judgement

— Your journal, a notebook, or a fresh piece of paper

— A pen that you love writing with

— Some kind of energetic tool, such as an essential oil, an energetic essence or spray, or a flower essence, oracle cards, crystals, white sage, sacred wood, or something else that you feel drawn to

— Somewhere comfortable to lie down after you go through this, to integrate the inner work if you'd like to, such as a yoga mat and/or bolster, a couch or your bed

— Perhaps a beautiful bunch of flowers nearby, a candle to light, incense to burn, and a mug of your favourite tea or coffee

And now the Forgiveness Movement step by step:

Step 1: Take a deep breath in. Ground and centre your energy. You have nowhere else to be, and nothing else to do doing. Be all here, now.

Step 2: Gather your notebook or journal and your pen, and sit with the following questions, answering them however feels good for you. Feel free to go off on tangents and write whatever else comes to you.

— What am I not forgiving myself (or someone else) for?

— Why am I holding onto this?

— What lessons have I learnt through this?

— Why do I think I can't let go?

— What do I need to know for my highest good? (Free write your answer to this one, without worrying about the answers coming through.)

— How would I love to feel, as I move forwards through forgiveness?

— What do I need to do or say to myself (or someone else), in order to forgive myself?

— Can I now give myself permission to forgive myself (or someone else)?

— What would forgiveness make space for?

— Is there another time, event or experience I need to forgive myself for? (If so, you may wish to go through some of the questions again.)

— Is there anything else I need to write about, or any other information, guidance or wisdom I need to receive, in order to move forward and forgive myself?

Step 3: Once you've gone through those questions and cleared your energy system through your writing, sit with the energy of what you've let go and of what you've created—newness, intentions, gratitude, expansion.

Step 4: If you feel like it, pick up your energetic tool of choice, and use it in a way that feels good for you. For example, if it's an oil, you can rub it on your heart space, throat, temples, wrists or wherever feels good. If it's an essence, drop it under your tongue. If it's a crystal, hold it in your hands or perhaps against an area of your body, eg. third eye, heart, solar plexus. Trust your intuition. Whatever feels right for you is right for you.

Step 5: Now sit or lie down, and breathe. Sit in this energy and with your intention and commitment to forgive yourself. Call it meditation, integration or grounding, or just sitting with yourself and your energy. Stay there for as long as you like.

Step 6: You may now wish to burn white sage or sacred wood to cleanse the space, or use an energetic room/body spray to shift old energy, or simply open the door or window and allow it to leave with love.

Step 7: Thank yourself, your energy, your inner guide, your higher self, and your guidance. Thank yourself for what you've just given yourself permission to do.

Step 8: Come back into your body, to the present time, and move on with your day.

Feel free to return to this Forgiveness Movement at any time, and as many times as you need. I had to do a lot of inner clearing and forgiveness work to move past my sense of failure. Remember, if you berate yourself for needing to forgive yourself, you're doubling your (inner) workload.

We grow by letting go affirmation

*I let go to surrender to where I am. I let go to flow. I trust
that a state of flow is always available to me. I stay in
my flow so that beautiful opportunities can come to me,
and I stay open to beautiful possibilities coming to me.
I allow forgiveness to resonate through my entire being
and energy system, knowing I am worthy of this.*

chapter 13

YOUR COMPASS BACK HOME

W ith forgiveness comes acceptance. Remember a while back we spoke about the 'what-ifs?' Let's go back to that for a second.

Is there a situation you've recently experienced that you keep running through in your mind, on repeat and repeat and repeat? You run yourself through every scenario of how it could have gone down differently. You say all the 'ifs, whens and buts' possible. You think through what you could have said, what you should have said or what you shouldn't have said. You berate yourself for what's already happened, draining yourself in the process.

This kind of self-criticism has no benefit, no reward and no purpose. But we so often find ourselves stuck there, because we think it's how we'll learn not to do it again. And maybe that's true, but another possibility is that we're human and we learn human mistakes and lessons in a very human way.

By accepting your situation, or the past situation, you're not necessarily agreeing with what happened. You're not condoning poor behaviour on your part or on another's part, and you're not lowering your standards. You're simply saying: 'This is what's already happened, and I am going to accept it for what it is.'

It has already happened, so please accept it. It'll actually be so much easier once you do. Stop going around and around in your head, stop chewing it over so much that it becomes more complicated than it needs to be. It has happened. Please, accept it. It's time to move on so you can fully heal, grow and thrive.

— Acceptance and forgiveness —

Are they the same thing? For me they feel different, but equally important in this surrendering process. I've been trying to consciously work out which comes first (ah, the old 'chicken and the egg' debate), and then I realised the answer is not a conscious one. It's formed through guidance and spirit and your sub-conscious. It's formed through whatever you need more of, most of, in this moment.

Sometimes we must forgive before we accept, and sometimes we find ourselves needing to accept before we can forgive. Let this be something that is fluid and tender in your heart. Let this process be something that isn't linear, because how can it be?

I truly believe we need to let go a little, in order to open up a lot more. I truly believe that if you fold the corner of this page down (so as to remember your place), and then flick through the book and land on a random page, that page will contain a piece of information you need today. Try it, now. Go on.

Then come back here to this page and remind yourself that life is not linear; that you don't need to be walking in a straight line to get to where you need to be; that you don't need to even know where you're going to get to where you want to be.

Our stories are our stories but they don't have a perfect beginning, middle and end. They end in the middle and they start at the end all the time. So can I answer the question of what comes first, acceptance or forgiveness? No, I can't. Because some days they are so interwoven it's as though they are the same, and some days they are so different, it's like comparing sugar and salt.

Some days they feel easy, and some days they feel hard. But they are a part of a surrendered, peaceful, beautiful life. Acceptance and forgiveness are your compass back home to your soul, where you truly believe that **everything will be okay.**

While self-compassion is the bridge to self-acceptance, here are a couple of tools to help you more easily and joyfully release guilt, grief and regret, and align yourself to acceptance, forgiveness, recalibration, surrender and more.

— Rose quartz for acceptance —

When it comes to acceptance, I love to work with rose quartz. It is a beautiful, light-pink crystal that relates to the heart chakra, our centre of acceptance (and love and forgiveness, of course).

When I say 'work with' this crystal, that can be as simple as keeping it near you throughout the day, holding it throughout meditation, and perhaps even keeping it next to your bed while you sleep.

— Oracle and angel cards —

Oracle cards are a beautiful way to tap into a deeper emotional state that is perhaps not sitting on the surface.

I remember a period of real confusion and overwhelm in my life, where one of the only things I could do to help me feel calmer each day was to pull my cards. I didn't do it from a state of stress though (I don't think that's helpful). I made sure to ground myself and my energy beforehand, by taking some deep breaths and journaling some of my stresses down, so I felt lighter before pulling the cards.

I'd then jot down the insights and guidance that came through from the card readings, and weave it through my own story and energetic vibration, so I could make sense of what I was feeling. I'd also write down the cards I pulled each day in my daily planner. That was a really nice way of tracking my week and it gave me a gentle purpose and focus each day, when I was feeling a little overwhelmed and overwrought. I can highly recommend this simple practice.

How to use oracle and angel cards:

— Take some deep, calming breaths.

— Open your journal and write out what's on your mind. Be as general or specific as you want; just write something down that feels good to get out.

— Take your deck of cards of choice, give them three taps with your knuckles (or three taps on the table or floor) to clear the energy of your last reading, and then pull a card. A one-card pull will give you a nice indication of where you're at in this present moment. If more than one card falls out of the deck, go with all of them. You can also pull three cards; the first one speaks of the energy of where you've come from (over the past few weeks or months), the second card is where you're presently at, and the third card speaks of the future or coming few weeks or months, giving you a nice idea of where to focus yourself and your energies.

I don't recommend doing three card readings every day, in case you end up with too much to focus on. Every few weeks or months is recommended, or at big junctures of change in your life. But of course, always do what feels good for you.

If you'd like to be consistent with your card readings, you can of course. I usually pull a card each week, and sometimes during the day or before or after a journaling session. I also like to pull a new card at the beginning of each new work project and month. But as I said, do what feels good to you. That's your primary purpose.

The acceptance affirmation

I am okay exactly where I am. I deeply and fully accept what has already happened, so I am able to open up to what may still be. I love and honour myself, and whoever else is involved in this situation. I accept what has happened, and where I am now. I am ready to take the lessons and move on. I am ready. I am safe. I accept.

---

chapter 14

DIVE UNDERNEATH

---

*Something amazing happens when
we surrender and just love.
We melt into another world, a realm of power already
within us. The world changes when we change.
The world softens when we soften. The world
loves us when we choose to love the world.*

MARIANNE WILLIAMSON

There's a scene in the movie *Dr Strange* where The Ancient One (played by Tilda Swinton) is talking to Dr Strange (played by Benedict Cumberbatch):

Ancient One: *You cannot beat a river into submission. You have to surrender to it.*

Dr. Strange: *I have to give up control to gain it? That doesn't make sense.*

Ancient One: *Not everything does.*

It might not always make sense to surrender and let go of our need to control, but in doing so we take a leap of faith into the supportive powers of something higher than ourselves. It feels so good to know we aren't the only ones carrying our destiny, we aren't the only ones holding ourselves up.

— Surrender and you'll find your power —

Trusting ourselves and the universe is one of our greatest allies. It can be our biggest support and the best foundation on which to build our best lives. One of the absolutely greatest ways to tune into that trust is to open into surrender.

Surrendering to where you are is not giving up. To me, it feels like the opposite; it feels like giving yourself permission to use what you've got, and to start where you are. And starting where you are is really the best place to begin.

— Starting to surrender —

Surrendering is about accepting ourselves, as well as all parts of our journey.

I invite you to approach this chapter with an open heart and mind, so that when it comes time for you to begin the slow and steady (or quick and steep) dive into your process of surrendering, you'll be as ready as you could ever be.

— Let yourself be here, now —

We like to fight the idea of surrendering, because it can feel safer to stay stuck than to let go into the unknown. However, the best part of letting go into surrender is that we get to build new ground. As we'll get onto soon, up-levelling our energy is a huge benefit of picking ourselves up after a failure, and of increasing our resilience. To do this, we must surrender through a struggle to allow it to pass through us sooner.

To surrender, you don't need to have already 'arrived' at your destination. Be here, now. Surrendering will help you move through what you're going through sooner, and you'll become more aligned, balanced and clear in the process.

— **How to surrender, even when you don't know how** —
There isn't one right way to surrender, and there isn't a wrong way to surrender. But what you'll find is that the more you resist it, the stronger the urge to surrender becomes. Sometimes it feels so strong that we mistake it for something else and we can feel panicky, like we're rushing to a destination we're not sure of yet.

So I believe it's imperative to take a few steps towards surrendering. They're mostly what you've already done in the lead-up to being here now, through reading this book. But there's one thing you may not have done yet. You may not have given yourself express permission to surrender, because maybe a part of you thinks you don't know how, or that surrendering means giving up. Giving up is a frightening thing, because it feels as though you're undoing all the hard work you've done until now.

But there's another side to this, and it's beautiful. Surrendering helps you move forward because it's a deep and true acceptance of who you are, of where you are, and of why you're here, even if you don't know all of those answers yet. The answers aren't what you need right now. Permission to surrender is what counts.

— Don't think about it too much —

Although this book is steeped in supporting you to surrender, I'm going to ask you to not think about it too much. In other words, don't overthink your surrendering process. Don't map it out and draw a Venn diagram and plan out every moment. Don't think it's something you can tick off a list (even though that's always fun!). That's not how surrendering works. That's when we think we've let go, but we're still attached. It's when we think our energy is aligned, but we're creating more stress through our obsessive thinking. And often when we invest too much energy into not being attached to something, we strengthen the bonds holding us to it.

Here's the secret sauce to surrendering: try not to work out the formula. Trying to control how you surrender is the opposite of surrendering, and I think that's where so many of us get tripped up. Controlling our surrendering creates suffering, and when we're picking ourselves up from a failure, we don't need to make ourselves suffer more.

So stop punishing yourself for not knowing—you're not supposed to—and start by simply showing up for yourself with love and respect, with generosity of spirit and with devotion.

You'll find your own secret sauce for surrendering and it'll be absolutely delicious.

— Step back into your surrender —

Sometimes we think the process of surrendering is like watching paint dry. Or bread become toast. Or grass grow. Or water boil. You get my point. We put all our effort and energy into surrendering, which makes it feel snail-paced, dull and forced. It's the only place we look.

Instead, we need to distribute energy evenly into other places in our lives too.

When you're finding it hard to surrender, how do you feel? Stressed, tight, stuck and forced come to my mind. So, if you're finding it hard to surrender and you keep trying to surrender, are you not putting more effort into your stress, your tension, your tightness or your stuckness?

What about coming at it from a different angle of release, of ease, of flow, of ... not trying so hard to surrender? It is easier to surrender than it is to fight; isn't that kind of the point? I don't think it's surrendering that's always so hard. It's the step before that gets us: letting go.

To let go is to trust. To let go is to offer up to something higher and ask for support.

Let's go for a reframe here. We can't control our lives anyway, so if we're just **living** aren't we already in a state of surrender? It's when we try to force and control that we step out of surrender and, in the stepping out, we feel as though we've lost control. So step back into your surrender; it's your natural state of being.

— Making space —

To make space to surrender is to clear your energy and prepare for a new, calming and grounding energy and vibration.

It's not the same as preparing and planning and taking action—surrender is not about action, remember? This is a time to go inwards, a time to settle your energy and your thoughts, a time to reflect and recharge, before a new wave of clarity and insight washes over you and through you.

And yes, this wave will come when you're ready, and not a moment sooner.

— Allow it to feel easier —

Surrendering can be as easy or as hard as you want it to. I choose ease. What do you choose? What do you need to do in order to ground into where you are now, even if you're not where you want to be yet? Apart from embracing trust and patience, apart from knowing you are guided and supported and loved, is there anything else you need to do? What if I suggested you don't need to do more? What if I suggested you just sit, and be?

Make the time—a simple five minutes a day—to sit with yourself. I don't mind what you call it, meditation or not, but this is what'll help you find it easier to surrender. You're not calling quits on yourself by letting yourself surrender, you're calling quits on your suffering and pain. You're saying to yourself: 'I see you, and you're okay. I see you, and I'm willing to be here for you. I see you, and I see the suffering, and I see the pain, but I don't need to attach to it. I can surrender to being here because in doing so, I trust I can then move on, and move up.'

— The waves —

I've always grown up near the ocean. I spent my childhood summers on the cape of South Africa with my family, and home has mostly been near the beach in Sydney. This has meant I've swum in the ocean a lot (except right after I watched *Jaws* with my cousins when I was fourteen!).

I've learnt that one of the best ways to swim through a wave that's a little bigger than expected is to take a deep breath and dive right underneath it, to the bottom of the ocean floor. You feel the waves roiling above you, the pressure of the water, and the strength of the ocean as you shift and stir forwards and then backwards with the wave overhead. And then, when it settles and the wave crashes onto the shore, you can come back up for air. Stronger for being able to weather the wave, softer for being able to be patient while it crashed around you, and a little bit delighted at where you find yourself.

When you feel you need to fight yourself or your surroundings, imagine you're diving under a wave. Take a deep, slow, powerful breath. Look around you and remember what everything looks like now. Dive underneath, let yourself flow with the undercurrent, trusting you have enough oxygen and that you'll be okay. Then come back up when the time feels right; when there's less pressure, less crashing around you. Take a deep breath, wipe the salty water from your eyes (tears, sweat or ocean) and take a look around. The world might look a little different now, and you'll be all the better for it.

— **You already know how** —

What about those times when it feels as though we're 'doing everything right' but still not achieving what we want to achieve, or getting to where we want to be? This is when it's not about doing more … it's about being here, surrendering to where we are. It's about still showing up and taking inspired, aligned action, but not gripping so tightly that we lose ourselves in the process.

Surrendering to where we are supports us in moving through the harder times with more ease; helping us through difficulties in our lives, when our egos want us to do more. Instead, we must remind ourselves to tune into our hearts and simply be more: more compassionate, more present, more grounded.

Surrendering isn't about doing, or we'd all be able to do it effortlessly. Mostly, surrendering is about shifting your mindset and your energy. It's about not fighting with where you are today, and with who you are today. It's about knowing you are enough, and trusting that everything will be okay.

When we don't allow ourselves to surrender, we aren't just trying to shut out pain. Inevitably, we end up shutting out pleasure too, because all of our available energy reserves are being focused towards this thing we don't want to feel.

We aren't even sure what it is that we don't want to feel but … my gosh … do we resist it! I believe it takes much more time and energy to not surrender, than to surrender. It's just that starting the process of letting it all go can feel so daunting, but once we start and can see the beauty, we can continue.

I think that the more you can let life guide you, the more you will enjoy your life and yourself. You won't fight with yourself or others as much. You won't worry about the future so much. You will be able to acknowledge if you're sliding back into a control mentality and you'll have the skills, foresight and ability to tune back into flow, surrender, gratitude and abundance. There is enough trust in this world for you. There is enough surrender in this world for you. There is enough time and enough flow. There is enough momentum and enough gratitude. It's all available for you, because it's already inside you.

I believe you already know how to surrender; you were born doing it. You forgot how to do it because so many of us are taught to control things, to stay in line, to colour inside the lines, to do the usual thing and go the usual route.

But you can be an adventurer and be grounded, you can surrender and discover who you are. You can do all of those things, you can be who you want to be. But first you must relinquish control over what you think should happen, when you think it should happen, and why you think it should happen your way, in your time, on your own terms.

Yes we can lead and live a bold life 'on our own terms'— that's a popular expression that finds its way onto social media accounts all over the world, and it's lovely, don't get me wrong. But living life on your own terms doesn't mean you control it. In fact, it's the opposite. It means you live in integrity and alignment, taking action towards your dreams, being in flow. It doesn't mean you live with rigidity and in control.

Questions to explore:
— *What does it mean to me to surrender?*
— *What do I think I'd be giving up by surrendering?*
— *What would I really lose by surrendering and letting go?*
— *What do I think I could gain by surrendering and letting go?*
— *What does it mean to me to live life on my own terms?*
— *What could I let go of to help make this come true for me?*
— *Finish this sentence: I can let life guide me by ...*

— Surrendering to the little things —

Of course, surrendering to the big things in life is important, but you'll also find there'll be little things for you to surrender to, sometimes every day.

At my yoga studio, there are little stickers of the studio's logo placed in equal spacing on the wooden floor. When experienced yogis come to practise, they know to place their mats down on the floor in the space between two stickers so that—should the studio fill up—every student has an equal space around their mat. No-one would be squished, and no-one would have more space than they need. We would all fit together, like a beautiful game of yogi tetris.

Except not everyone puts their mats down in this way. Should you enter the yoga studio and need to find a spot, sometimes you have to ask a fellow yogi to move their mat over. Sometimes they look at you as if you've asked them to give you a lock of their hair, and sometimes they smile, nod in agreement and quickly shuffle over. A few times, when someone has looked at me like I'm the most annoying person on the planet, I've gently pointed to the stickers and explained how they work—not to be the most annoying person on the planet, just to save them time next class!

This morning in yoga, people had spread their mats out so much that our teacher had to go around and ask people to shuffle over to fit more mats in. For a few moments, people stared at her blankly—you could almost see their minds ticking over, wondering how you could possibly fit more yoga mats into the row. And then a few people got up, moved their mats just a few inches and these empty spaces appeared like magic!

It seemed so much harder to do before they tried. And it seemed so much harder until a few people got the message that it was okay to move, to make space, to try something new. All of a sudden, two more yoga mats could fit into a space which moments before had seemed full. All of a sudden, making space seemed so much easier. And hopefully, all of a sudden, people realised that exploring your own space and getting closer to the 'uncomfortable' can be a wonderful exploration into who you are.

Some people find it uncomfortable to be close to others, so they want to keep their space. Sometimes people are so in their own space, that they enter the quiet cave of a yoga studio, and instead of gently and quietly rolling their mats out, they fling them out and—like the crack of a whip in an old Western movie—their mat flies through the air, only to land on the floor with a thud, shaking the energy around them with the very clear message: 'I am not here yet, I am still in my head.'

My all-time favourite example of 'I am not here yet, I am still in my head' is when I arrived at yoga to hear the sound of bells. It wasn't a cat, no. It was a fellow yogi, wearing an anklet with bells on. At yoga. Sharing space. I'm not proud to say that my patience ran out before class had even started. My inner yogi tried to stay calm, while all around me I saw the other students glancing around the room, trying to find the source of this jingling, jangling sound. I glanced at the teacher, who's a friend, mouthed where the sound was coming from and the teacher played louder, calming music throughout class.

The point is, the call to surrender can be big and loud, or a soft whisper, and that is okay. Sometimes in the surrender journey, we are faced with situations that truly call on us to surrender, in the most random situations. The morning I went to yoga with the bell anklet lady, I had been craving a peaceful, quiet practice. But the universe had other plans. Bells! Sound! Ringing! Unpredictable! I was called to breathe, and to be very much surrendering to where I was.

The irony was not lost on me. I hope it's not lost on you, if or when you too find yourself in a situation that feels almost too comical in its suggestion that you surrender if you're feeling tightly wound. Perhaps you need to start something again, if the first time wasn't actually feeling great (like making a breakfast you don't really want to be eating and then burning it); or go slower if you've been rushing (like when you always catch the red traffic lights when you're in a hurry).

Not everyone will act like you. Not everything will go your way. This is life, and that is okay. Make peace with it, as best you can, as often as you can, and then get back to making space for yourself to fit between the things that do feel good for you. Surround yourself with as much peace and positivity as you can.

— Leaning into surrender —

Surrendering is not about doing. It's about being. Sometimes this concept feels hard to grasp, because so many of us love doing! We love taking action, getting organised, and making stuff happen. We like the idea of controlling, of being in control. We don't like the idea of surrendering, because isn't that like giving up? Isn't that like saying we don't care what happens to us anymore and we're just going to let ourselves go?

The truth is, that's not the truth but our fear—our ego, our inner critic—trying to make us believe that. Staying stuck in fear and confusion sometimes—only initially though—feels easier than moving and flowing into surrender.

To surrender to where we are is to stop fighting and start flowing. To surrender to where we are is to let what needs to be brought to the surface come to light, so we can let it go, and feel even lighter and clearer because of it, not in spite of it.

You can't **do more** to surrender. You have to feel it. It's a feeling to let go of, not hold onto. And while sometimes there are beautiful actions which we can align ourselves to on our journey to surrendering, quite often it's when we step back from the doing that we allow ourselves to flow, float, be, breathe and receive.

Sometimes surrendering means giving up something that isn't working for you, in order to make space for something better ... even though you have no idea what that might be. Surrendering can mean showing up, stepping up, and living up to our full potential. It's not about backing down and giving up. It's about accepting and flowing and being okay with not knowing.

The surrender affirmation

I let go. I surrender to where I am right now. I know it's
safe to surrender, and I know I'm capable of doing so.
I allow myself to surrender, so that I can step more fully
and freely into my power, clear and ground my energy, and
be completely present in my life; here, now, today.

chapter 15

FEELING GOOD

Do you remember at the beginning of the book that I mentioned I got really sick, twice, in the year I was learning how to truly surrender? Well in hindsight, I can see this was actually my body processing what I was going through, and healing from it.

I think I got so sick because I was suppressing so much, out of fear of looking at it. I think I felt overwhelmed at the mistaken notion that I somehow had to start again (when really, I'd made so much progress by failing), and my body had had enough.

Even more than that, I can look back now and see that I didn't give myself permission to let go, and that's why I got sick. I kept doing the forgiveness work, but I don't think I really forgave myself. Whenever I had the energy for it, I kept trying to create my own momentum again; but as soon as something slightly unexpected threw me off my path, instead of just getting back on my proverbial horse, I gave myself a hard time about it, and took another step back.

I kept trying to understand the reasons behind my perceived failure, so I could try to avoid the same mistakes. What I needed to do was love myself for making them anyway, and learn the lessons instead. The reasons don't matter if you ignore the lessons; the teachings are what counts.

Getting sick was my body's way of showing me where to look. The lungs are an energetic container for guilt, grief and regret when under emotional stress or strain; when healthy, they are a mirror of how we're going with the flow, breathing easily, letting go and allowing ourselves to receive. My body was guiding me to see where the problem really was. The problem wasn't that I'd failed. The problem was that I wasn't forgiving myself for it, and then allowing myself to deeply and fully heal and move on.

Mostly, it was all stuck in my lungs. Mostly, I was feeling regretful and aggrieved, grieving and finding it so hard to let go. Grieving the loss of what I'd thought I'd wanted (and thought I'd 'deserved'); grieving the perceived loss of my dreams and my path; grieving the perceived loss of my identity that had been so wrapped up in my ambition and goals (see how this is all about my perception?); and grieving the idea that I'd fallen so far. (Drama, Cass! Everything was really and truly okay.) I had pushed myself so much, so far and so hard, that my body, my breath and my lungs were struggling to keep up.

When I got sick, there were so many beautiful natural remedies I turned to. Although I did, at one stage, need to take a course of antibiotics as—due to my history of asthma—it became painful to breathe (which is obviously scary!). I continued to take my immune and respiratory herbs too, and to engage in slow and intentional breathing exercises through yoga. Thankfully, there came a day where it became easier and easier to breathe (in the literal, emotional and energetic sense).

So, in this chapter, we'll go through some natural ways you can lift your mood, increase your energy and clear the mental fog that can sometimes accompany disappointment, guilt, grief and regret.

— The mental fog —

Through my days before the Great Surrender (ha!), it often felt like I was in a great big mental fog of disappointment, fear and anxiety. Have you felt like that after a disappointment or failure? It feels like it creeps up on us, and sometimes like it'll never let go, but of course we can let it go (and naturally).

I dug into my own natural healing toolkit to clear my fog and tune into my flow, and I hope the following tools will help you too.

(Please note: I've given a long list of herbs to take but, of course, that doesn't mean you have to take them all. Make an appointment with a naturopath or herbalist, or pop into your local health food store and ask to speak to a naturopath or herbalist, if you want to try taking some herbal medicine. Don't ask to speak to a nutritionist if you want to try herbs, as they can help you with food and nutritional medicine suggestions, but not herbal medicine. A naturopath or herbalist can give you some extra healing tips and suggest specific herbs, dosages, brands and products. When taking herbal medicines, you can take them in tea, tablet, liquid or powder form. Of course, you can add many of them to your cooking.)

To help energise your body and heal your adrenal glands, reach for herbs such as Licorice and Rehmannia as a start, as well as herbs that have adaptogenic properties (to help your body adapt to stress and heal from fatigue) such as Rhodiola, basically any ginseng (Siberian, Korean, American and Indian Ginseng, which is also known as Withania), Echinacea, Shatavari, magnesium and vitamin C, acupuncture, less coffee, less sugar, less alcohol, plenty of healthy foods, fluids and rest.

Give your body time to adjust and heal; fatigue isn't something you can just sleep off in one good night's rest. If you've been pushing your body for months, slow down and go inwards now. Create self-care rituals, create boundaries and then honour them with love.

To help clear mental fog, balance and lift your mood, reach for green tea, dark chocolate (yay!), and herbs such as Rhodiola, Siberian ginseng, Licorice, St John's Wort (not to take if you're on the contraceptive pill or most medications), Schisandra, Skullcap, Vervain, Turmeric, Oats, Withania and Rosemary as well as the nutrients zinc, vitamin D, magnesium, fish oils and the B vitamins.

To improve your immune system (and support your respiratory system), take the herbs Echinacea, Andrographis, Mullein, Thyme, Elecampane, Grindelia, Fennel, Licorice, Ginger, Siberian Ginseng, Cat's Claw, and the nutrients zinc and vitamin C. It can also be nice to diffuse the essential oils of eucalyptus leaf and peppermint, and/or dilute them in a carrier oil, such as sweet almond oil, and rub them on your chest. Add some lavender for its calming benefits.

To help ease anxiety, restlessness and insomnia, reach for the beautiful herbs Passionflower, Rehmannia, Oats, Lavender, Valerian, Vervain, Zizyphus, Lemon Balm, Chamomile, Motherwort, Withania, American Ginseng, magnesium and B vitamins.

To help reduce the sugar cravings that can accompany low moods, reach for the herb Gymnema or the mineral chromium (they're often used together in sugar-balancing formulas) to help cut the cravings naturally. Adding cinnamon to your diet is also great. If you find yourself craving sugar as a way to temporarily lift your mood, make sure you're eating a wholesome diet and not skipping meals. Eat well, and support your mood and nervous system naturally.

To help get out of your head and into your body, reach for journaling, kinesiology, meditation and exercise. I don't know where I'd be without my journal during those tough times. You don't necessarily have to write in your journal daily to benefit, but having a container for your thoughts is more powerful than you know. Don't overthink what and when you write—the most important thing is that you understand and honour how powerful it is, so that making space to do it becomes a natural part of your healing and releasing process.

— **Do what you can** —

Do you have to do all of those things every day to heal your mind, body and spirit? Of course not. Now is not the time to put pressure on yourself or impose a time limit on healing from the physical, mental, emotional and spiritual side effects of rising and recalibrating from failure and disappointment. Do what you can, with what you've got.

And remember, feeling good about how you're looking after your body is important too. If you start to feel pressured, let something go, or have a nap. Most things seem better after a nap.

Healing affirmation

I allow myself to deeply heal and move on, in ways that feel supportive to me. I allow myself to fully breathe out and let go of guilt, grief and regret.

YOU ARE STILL HERE,

AND THERE IS STILL TIME.

———

#itsallgoodbook

chapter 16

CHANGE YOUR TUNE

Don't despair: despair suggests you are in
total control and know what is coming.
You don't—surrender to events with hope.

ALAIN DE BOTTON

I used to think I was the dud at restaurants. No matter who I went out to dine with, I would be the one whose food would be forgotten, or it would come late to the table, or there would be a bug in it. And lo and behold, this happened to me more often than not. It got to the stage where I'd shrug my shoulders and roll my eyes when it happened, as if to say 'Well, of course it happened to me!' My family took to constantly reminding me that I wasn't the dud, and that it happened to me so often because I was so focused on being the dud.

I didn't believe this of course, until one day I got so sick of it that I changed my tune. I stopped telling myself and others that I was the dud at every cafe and restaurant I went to. I stopped expecting to be the dud. I stopped shrugging my shoulders and rolling my eyes. I stopped expecting the worst, and started being hopeful for the best, yet staying neutral about the outcome. And what do you know? My food started to arrive alongside my family and friends' meals, and I stopped finding bugs in my salad. Go me!

I think you probably already know a thing or two about 'perceived failures'—those situations from your past that didn't go the way you'd planned. I truly believe those moments are really diamonds in the rough (even if they bring with them some really tough times). I know that if you stay stuck in an energy of perceived failure, then riding the waves of surrender, acceptance and forgiveness, and rising back up, feels much harder and further away.

When you're in the state of thinking you've done something wrong, something bad, something from which you can't come back, then where is your self-worth, your self-esteem, your self-confidence? It's so far away that it doesn't even feel like it's a part of you anymore. It feels so unavailable and almost alien to you. So calling it back to you is your challenge.

Your challenge, your mission, your initiation is to let go of your identity as a failure, and tune back into the core of who you are; the core of who you are who knows deeply that you are not a failure.

Maybe a situation hasn't gone exactly to (your) plan. Maybe a part of you is finding the current situation really hard to reconcile with your dreams, your plans, your aims and intentions. Maybe it feels like where you are really sucks, and I'm so sorry about that.

I'm so sorry if you feel stuck. I'm so sorry if things didn't go the way you wanted them to. I'm so sorry if what you want feels so far away.

But that doesn't mean that you can't still aim higher, that you can't still get to where you want to be, or that you can't still be who you want to be (all the while knowing that **you are enough**, exactly as you are right now). You are still here, and there is still time. You still have time to do things differently, to learn from where you are, and to accept this mission of knowing deeply that you haven't done anything wrong—that you will be okay.

We're about to move into recalibrating from all these insights and changes and then up-levelling our energy, thoughts, beliefs and mindset. To do so, you have to be 100 percent willing, ready and able to move on.

Are you willing? Are you ready? Because I know for sure you're able!

***

Change your tune affirmation

I know I can change my perspective, and I am ready, willing and able to do so. I allow in hope, lightness and joy.

***

DON'T BREAK THE SHADOW OUT

OF YOU; BEND WITH IT.

#itsallgoodbook

chapter 17

BEND OR BREAK

When we feel stuck in the fight that comes with not surrendering, we have a choice: to bend to where we are, or to break. Sometimes breaking feels easier in the moment, because we think if we create more pain out of our current discomfort, then the first pain will dissipate, right? It gives us something to hold onto, even though it's not what we really want.

I know I sometimes felt like I was losing my cool, when I felt stuck for so long. I would create pockets of movement and momentum but they never felt like they stuck with me for long. Why? I think I wasn't bending enough; I was still stuck in my ways, because I didn't believe I could find my flow again.

But in reality, I had to un-know what I knew. I had to look at my situation with a beginner's mind. I had to allow myself to see it all from a new, fresh and open perspective. Instead, my mind kept me stuck, which meant my energy was stuck, which meant I kept telling myself, 'I told you so.'

It's time for you to bend, or break. Bending is surrendering, it's saying: 'I'm ready to see things in a new light, and that includes my shadow self.' Perhaps part of surrendering is so hard because we don't want to see our shadows. We are taught to always look towards the light, grow towards the light, and rise towards the light.

But what is light without a few shadows? To surrender is to remind yourself that your shadow self is as beautiful and worthy and necessary as your light.

Your light is nothing without a shadow, so lean into it. Don't break the shadow out of you; bend with it.

— Un-know it —

Stuckness is a mentality; we choose to think we know the answer and so we don't see new possibilities. We say 'I told you so' instead of 'Let's see where this goes.'

Welcome in your beginner's mind. What do you know and why do you think you know it? How can you un-know it?

— You've changed —

Heraclitus, a Greek philosopher famous for his assertion that change is the fundamental essence of the universe, is known to have said: *No man ever steps in the same river twice, for it's not the same river and he's not the same man.*

You can never walk into the same river twice because of flow, because of change, because we are not meant to stay the same, and neither is the river of your life.

Don't try to stop the flow just to work out why you're here or to understand the mistakes you've made. Pick up your bags and keep on walking; you can work it out on the way.

Bend or break affirmation

I'm ready to see things in a new light. I'm ready to flow to where I need to go.

YOU HAVE A NEW MAP NOW; TRUST IN ITS
NEWNESS, ITS ROADS AND BOUNDARIES,
ITS LAKES AND RIVERS, ITS MOUNTAINS
AND VALLEYS. TRUST IN ITS BEAUTY.

#itsallgoodbook

part 2

THE MIDDLE

DURING YOUR RECALIBRATION

---

chapter 18

THERE'S A NEW MAP

———

Do you remember when I told you the story at the beginning of the book, of how my husband and I went to the yin yoga and sound healing evening? For me, there was more to it than just having a beautiful and calming yoga experience. During the event, we did a lot of 'call and response' singing, while one of the hosts played an instrument. While that's something I can sometimes be uncomfortable about, on that night I decided to just roll with it.

My husband used to sing at school and university, and has a wonderful voice, (he even surprised me and sang to me at our wedding!), so he jumped right into the singing. After a moment, I followed. The vibe of the night was so grounding and calming, and I quickly found myself loving the singing. After several minutes, I started to sink more fully into myself. It felt as though I'd lost track of time, of others in the room (except my hubby and his beautiful voice), and certainly of any lingering self-consciousness.

It was then that I started to feel really emotional, and tears started to stream down my face. All of a sudden, it felt as though I was singing through the cracks of my failure, singing through the hard few months I'd had the year previously, and it felt as though with each breath, with each octave, with each decibel, I was releasing and clearing more and more of it.

Through singing and using my voice—essentially, clearing and balancing my throat chakra—I was expelling guilt and grief. I could feel it. I could sense these layers—the joy of releasing, and the pain of the failure underneath it—and I kept up the singing ... until my throat closed up.

My throat suddenly felt constricted and I couldn't sing anymore. I took a sip of water, and then another. I cleared my throat with a cough, and then another. I tried to sing again, but literally no sound came out.

Have you ever had one of those dreams where you try to scream but nothing comes out? That's what it felt like. I put my hands on my throat, and then on my heart space, and took some deep, calming breaths. I started to hum in response to the singing. I kept reminding myself—my physical, mental, emotional and spiritual self—that I was okay, that I was forgiven, that I was moving forwards, and that everything would be okay. I trusted the signs my body was giving me—that there was still some lingering pain—and in return I sent it love, and compassion. I let my being know, with everything I had, that it was safe to let go, to recalibrate, to move forward again.

And after a few more moments of feeling uncomfortable, of having lost my voice, of having felt that I could affect no change, and of then moving slowly, slowly (through soft humming) back to a space of empowerment, I found my voice—and started singing—again.

— Uncomfortable is okay —

You know how sometimes, if you're having a shaky, uncomfortable, stuck-in-your-head day (the opposite of those grounding, peace-filled days), it feels as though things are crumbling down around you? And sometimes, even when we want to step up into a new atmosphere of our being to a new level—when we can see that we've maybe fallen and we know that now is the time to stand back up again—in those moments (or days, or weeks, or months) it sometimes feels like things are breaking down before we can build them back up.

This can feel uncomfortable. In these moments, we are the raw skin of a healing wound, out in the elements— the wind, the water, the earth, the fire, the air—without the protection of our old bandage. But uncomfortable is okay. Uncomfortable is how we stretch, how we grow.

— The lobster story —

A little while ago, a video started circulating about a rabbi taking us through the process of a lobster shedding its old, small shell, and growing a new one.

A lobster, happy in its shell for a while, will one day realise that shell is becoming too rigid, too tight, too uncomfortable. The lobster will find a rock, hide beneath it for protection, shed its old, small shell and grow a new, bigger one. The catalyst for the shedding of the old shell is that it's becoming uncomfortable; the lobster is growing, expanding. But in the space between the old and the new, the lobster is raw, vulnerable and exposed. It probably thinks it has no idea how to grow a new shell or when it will be finished, but it does it anyway. (#Goals)

This is like the process of growth and recalibrating before finding your new ground. What does it mean to recalibrate? It's about finding a new way home to yourself, a new path to your dreams, a bigger shell to fit the new, expansive you, and a new way to fly when those first wings you grew didn't quite make the cut, or could only lovingly take you so far.

— Embody the synonyms in your life —

I'm sure you know what a synonym is: a word or phrase that means the same (or almost the same) as another word or phrase. We can embody this wonderful word in our lives by amending our plans when the first plan doesn't work out, and finding a new way.

A friend and mentor once said to me, 'Imagine where you want to be is at the top of a mountain, and you don't quite know how you'll get there, but each path you take is a path that leads you to the top.'

When I look up synonyms for 'recalibrate' on Thesaurus. com (a writer's bestie, after coffee of course), I find *transmute, metamorphose, shift, change, develop, reshape, reconstruct, modify, adjust, amend, fine tune.*

To every single synonym I say: 'Yes! This is what we must go through, this is what we must embrace if we are to surrender, to heal, to rise and to trust that everything will be okay.'

If one path doesn't lead you to where you want to be, is there another path close by, that you could hop on over to?

Yes, there is. Is there a fork you can take that'll create the same meaning in your life, even though you're on a different path? Yes, there is.

The reason I'm talking about synonyms here is that they represent another path, another option, another step in the right direction. They help us to say something a few different ways, without repeating ourselves. They help us understand new words, by relating old information to words we already know.

They help us adapt and make sense of stories, keep things fresh. This is what you can do in your life, by acting mindfully and making good decisions when things don't go the way you initially wanted them to.

— Your new map —

What does it mean to recalibrate? It's to transform; it's to acknowledge that who you were 'before' is not who you are now, and to accept this.

To recalibrate is to reshape your thoughts, transform your inner processes, and modify the map you once thought you were following. You have a new map now; trust in its newness, its roads and boundaries, its lakes and rivers, its mountains and valleys. Trust in its beauty. Don't worry about what the old map used to look like; enjoy it for what it is today. Follow it with all your heart, and stay with it … until one day, the map changes again. And when it changes, trust that you'll absolutely be able to follow the new one; because you will.

You would've already done it before, and you'll be able to do it again.

— Your fall will become your rise —

Recalibration is the wet sand on the beach after a storm. The storm has come, and maybe done some damage; but it's gone now, and the sand on the beach will never look the same again. But it's still beautiful, and you can still build a castle out of it, using those tiny grains of sand that were something else—rocks and minerals, corals and shells.

To recalibrate is to modify your plans to fit this new mould of who you are, and to honour what you now want. Old relationships may disentangle themselves, and new ones may form. Old pieces of you may decide they no longer fit; yet when they break away, they make even more space for seamless growth.

Feeling into this sensation of recalibrating, transmuting, reshaping and adjusting is all part of the surrendering process.

Falling into this sensation is part of the surrendering process too. For if we never fall, we never learn how to pick ourselves up and put ourselves back together again. And without one, the other feels purposeless. If you trust that your fall will develop into a rise (with conscious choice, with courage, with integrity and with intention), then falling may not become easier, but it'll become more meaningful.

Likewise, falling makes our rises feel more purposeful. We become more mindful, because we want to remember this journey of expanding into ourselves and filling our lives with flow.

— Recalibration is your phoenix rising —

If I'd never fallen, I wouldn't be writing this book to you. If you'd never fallen, you wouldn't be reading it.

How can you start to recalibrate after a big disappointment, and integrate everything you've learnt? By being present. By showing up for yourself and saying: 'Okay, I'm ready; it's time to fit my pieces back together again and reshape the mould to something that feels more like me.' By trying new things, or old things with a new lens; by forgiving, accepting, and of course, by surrendering; by trusting yourself again (which sometimes becomes dimmer with a fall); by believing in yourself and your path; and by trusting that everything will be okay.

The recalibration meditation

Read the following meditation as many times you need to, until you feel some kind of shift, or a wave—or even a tiny stream!—of calm wash over you.

Take a deep breath in and out. Place your hands over your heart and settle into your skin. Repeat the following to yourself, out loud or in your mind, and then sit quietly for a little while, just breathing and being and recalibrating:

I am recalibrating with every breath in, and every breath out.

I am forming the new out of the old, and I am ready for it.

I release what I no longer need, and I let it go with love.

I know I am always reshaping my internal landscape, and I know this is okay.

I fine-tune my intentions; I know what I want.

I transmute old energy, and I open up to the new.

I am surrendering.

I am safe here, because I am where it is safe.

I am ready for the next step.

I am rising.

I am ready for the next step.

I am rising.

I am ready for the next step.

I am here.

chapter 19

BRAVO, BRAVO!

*A*fter we recalibrate, and before the next wave of sweet, sweet clarity rushes in (we'll go through that next), you might find yourself in a period of integration. This is where you can finally see the wood for the trees. This is where your hand finally touches the doorhandle of the next door, the one in the dark corridor that you couldn't see or sense for so long.

A higher perspective has made itself known to you (or rather you've made space to see it and you're finally ready to look), and you can see how you're integrating the lessons you've learnt, without feeling attached to any pain they used to contain.

When we are in an integration phase, we start to consciously receive new, clearer energies and ideas. New inspiration starts to make its way through the fog that held space for so long. The energy of the new, of creation, of building a new foundation; it's all here now. We integrate all aspects and layers of the lessons we've learnt. We know we're ready for growth, for the next stage, and we release any final elements that truly don't fit us anymore.

Put simply, you are taking all the information you gathered through your tough experience, your challenge, your difficult period, and you're using it to make new choices, to maintain your path or change track, to up-level your life and to continue to work towards your desires.

You've done it! See? You survived. There is another side. And you can see it now. Bravo, bravo!

Integration affirmation

I consciously receive new insights and ideas, and integrate these into my being. I allow myself to integrate all aspects and layers of my up-levelling. I am ready for growth. I'm ready for the next stage.

TRUST THAT OUT OF CHAOS,

YOUR CLARITY WILL COME.

#itsallgoodbook

chapter 20

SWEET, SWEET CLARITY

And just like every song I haven't heard yet,
no I didn't know the words in front of me.

GAVIN JAMES, *NERVOUS*

I've been going to pottery lately. When I started, I had to remind myself that it was okay to be a beginner again. I had to understand that when I throw my clay down on the wheel, while I might have an idea of what I want the final mug or bowl to look like (I haven't worked out how to make a plate yet), I can't see it yet. All I see in the beginning is a mound of clay—completely mouldable and moveable, but still just a lump of clay—and I have to keep my bigger vision in my sights, but also let the mug or bowl (and hopefully one day, a plate) become what it needs to become, or something better.

Mostly, my final pieces have looked better than I expected, not because I'm the most brilliant potter in the world, but because seeing what was once just a dream for the clay slowly become a tangible, solid object in my hands—seeing my dream come to fruition—is even sweeter than the dream of it.

If your time spent dreaming is sometimes sweeter than your goal becoming realised, you're chasing the rush of the unknown, perhaps even the rush itself—the planning and dreaming and scheming—and not the solid ground of your dreams and goals.

If you get to the end goal and don't feel anything, or you feel flat, or you wonder 'is this it?' then maybe you've been chasing for the sake of it, and not because you're focused on what you're making. Maybe you've been chasing external success, instead of internal fulfilment. Maybe you've not been reaching for the stars that you truly want to reach for, but for the ones you think you should be reaching for.

Instead of just chasing, ask yourself: 'What do I really want to make and create and receive in my life? How can I take action and make space to do this?' The process to make and open up to it is important, but so is the acknowledgement, awareness and pride when the goal actually becomes a reality.

The same can be said for so many of our dreams. We might not always know what the outcome will be, but we can stay centred with clarity and focus; we can invite our vision to stay (or come back), to keep us on track, to help us see clearly again, and to help us enjoy the whole ride.

— Clarity and purpose will return —

Even if you've felt your vision of your future has been foggy of late, please trust that there will be a time, after the pain and release, and the integrations and realisations, where your new goals become crystal clear. The period of mild confusion or intense overwhelm that preceded this ceases to be a big deal, because the sweet clarity that comes brings with it more pure possibility than you could have imagined.

The clarity you will receive is a confirmation that everything you went through has a bigger purpose, and that you're now ready to see that.

We have to trust that, just because we can't see the answer, it doesn't mean it's not there and already written in the stars for us. Clarity will come, and you'll be ready when it arrives.

— Out of chaos comes clarity —

If your inner world is feeling chaotic after a failure but before an energetic up-levelling (more on that soon), then you're onto a good thing. I know it doesn't always feel like it, but the chaos you're feeling is countless new waves of clarity you haven't mastered or understood yet. This new energy is still working out where it fits in your mind, body, spirit and soul.

Trust that out of chaos, your clarity will come.

— Focus on today —

You don't need all the answers this moment, but I've found a way to help soothe the stress if you think you need to know your future now: focus on today. Miraculous, right? Focus on now, on today, on this moment.

You don't need to know what to do next, because that moment hasn't come yet. Ground your energy into the now, get out of your head and into your body, and really feel the ground beneath your feet, the breath in your lungs and the sunshine on your face. Then you'll let go of the pressure (intrinsically or extrinsically placed) that says: 'You need to know all of your goals, and exactly where you're heading, all of the time.'

I put extra pressure on myself during the times I felt like I had no clarity on my future, because I didn't surrender to where I was, and I didn't give myself permission to just not know, for as long as I needed to not know. In a sense, at that first pottery lesson I was just looking at the lump of clay and wondering why it wasn't a perfectly-crafted bowl yet, and wondering how it was all going to work out. I needed to let go of the need to know the outcome, while I shaped what was in front of me into something that I loved.

Think of the clay from my pottery class as an analogy of my failure. If I had simply let myself see and trust that what felt like a mess was, in fact, a beautifully mouldable piece of possibility, would I have believed in my ability to shape it into something beautiful? Yes, because that's what I allowed myself to do when I made my second bowl.

If you closed your eyes right now, you'd still have a sense of where you are in the room, in time and space, in the universe of your own world. If your eyes feel shut to your bigger vision, that doesn't mean you're not on the right track.

If you don't know where you're meant to be going, why not be grounded and content and grateful where you are right now? Why not trust that just because you can't see your bigger vision, that doesn't mean it's not there?

— **Clarity of your future isn't your crystal ball** —
A client recently asked me: 'How can I have a clear vision of my future? Isn't that kind of like asking for a crystal ball?'

We can have a wonderful sense of clarity of our future, of where we're going and of where our aligned energy feels like it's moving, without needing to know all of the specifics, and without having the answers written down.

When you feel aligned to where you're going, and to where you currently are, you'll open doors you didn't previously see, ones you hadn't previously imagined.

When you feel aligned to where you're going, and to where you currently are, you won't feel like you've been energetically knocked over by a bus, if a challenge or a problem arises. You'll have the insight, energy, awareness and resilience to find a way around your obstacles, no matter what. Perhaps you'll go over them, or under them, or around them; it doesn't matter how you do it, because you'll be as aligned on the other side. You'll know that being challenged is actually wonderful, that failing is good, and that getting back up again is so very possible for you.

Give yourself permission to not know your answers and they'll come to you when they're ready to be seen, understood and applied.

— Make a space —

Have you ever had to consciously create a dream? Maybe, but probably not. So often our dreams, ideas and inspirations come to us—they arrive in the s p a c e s in between. So make some space and get between it. Allow your dreams, ideas and inspirations to arrive. They'll come when they're ready, and not a moment sooner.

Allow your clarity to arrive; it'll come when you're ready, and not a moment sooner. And it will come, I can promise you that. Look at all the beautiful healing work you've done up until this moment? Why **wouldn't** it come?

Don't ask the question: *Will I have a clear vision of my future again?* Instead, ask the question: *What can I do today, knowing my clarity will come?*

Act in your flow and your flow will find you. Act with clarity, and a crystal-clear vision will emerge through the foggy lens you've been squinting at.

You'll have all the information you need to move forwards, and you'll be ready, because you haven't forced it … you've allowed it. And that's the best way to see clearly.

— You have to go through it —

When I was growing up, one of my favourite children's books was *We're Going on a Bear Hunt* by Michael Rosen and Helen Oxenbury. In the book, little children go on a (pretend) bear hunt with their dad and meet all kinds of obstacles on their way, like a huge puddle of mud and a hedge, among other things.

Whenever they are confronted by an obstacle, they sing to each other: *We can't go over it; we can't go under it; we have to go through it!*

For some reason that line swirled its way through my mind often, when I found myself going through my period of heightened challenges. At times, I couldn't go over it (even though I wanted to tell myself, harshly, to 'get over it'), and there were times I couldn't go under it, nor around it … I had to go through it. And so do you.

The best thing to know is this: there is another side, and it's glorious and bright and grounded, and there's space for you here, when you're ready.

Sweet, sweet clarity affirmation

I open up to a beautiful and expansive vision of my
future. I allow clarity to wash over me and through me.
I trust exactly where I am, and where I am going.

WILL YOU BE READY TO LET GO

OF YOUR OLD LIMITS, EXPAND,

INTEGRATE AND UP-LEVEL?

OF COURSE YOU WILL.

OF COURSE YOU CAN.

THAT'S WHY YOU'RE HERE.

———

#itsallgoodbook

chapter 21

LEAD FROM YOUR HEART

n the moments and days and weeks between my old vision being released and my new vision coming to me, I felt really shaky and ungrounded. I was very 'in my head' and I needed constant grounding to stay out of it.

We get out of our bodies in the first place because we're overthinking. And overthinking—while it likes to trick us into thinking it's helpful—doesn't do much, I can tell you. (Coming from an overthinker over here.)

One day, I was 'future-tripping' and having a moment of major overthinking about a situation that hadn't even eventuated yet. I was talking about it with a girlfriend who said to me: 'When you overthink something, the only one who suffers is you.'

The truth of her comment was a welcome smack in the face, and I gladly accepted it. It was true; staying stuck in my head and overthinking wasn't helping me, nor was it helping anyone else. It wasn't speeding up time so that the event happened sooner, and it wasn't helping me feel more grounded or more confident in my ability to beautifully manage the situation. (While on some level, I knew that of course I could and would manage it perfectly, and everything really would be okay.)

So I made a very conscious effort to notice and acknowledge the overthinking, and to remind myself that worrying about something is not the same thing as taking action to make yourself or the situation feel better—whether that's by becoming more grounded and calm, or letting it go, or doing anything else that would actually help.

Worrying pulls you out of your body and into your head; it leaches precious personal power; it lessens trust in the self and the universe; it slows the process of letting go; and is the opposite of surrendering to where you are.

— Cut the cords of overthinking —

By doing the opposite of what your 'mind chatter' is telling you to do—by coming into your body—you'll see that you can let it go, you can cut the cords to your overthinking.

Yesterday, I was on a Skype call with a wonderful client, who is a self-professed overthinker. Our session—a business alignment coaching and kinesiology session—centred on her confidence in her work, offerings and skills. She said she'd been feeling very 'in her head' the last little while, overthinking and not really trusting herself enough.

During the session she had a light bulb moment; she told me that she could now see that she was shifting on from a negative spiral of self-doubt. She reflected on going through a really big learning curve, which contained some difficulties and some lessons; and she said that even though at the time she could see that the challenge was serving her, she now realised the point was to understand **how** it was serving her.

She could see that her self-doubt had been trying to keep her safe, because if, after her challenges, she never tried again, she wouldn't have to risk failing and not being perfect again. She would be 'safe' from failure, but still stuck in self-doubt.

Her self-doubt had previously been keeping her exactly where she was because she would doubt herself and her abilities, instead of taking action. She could see this had been a pattern in her life, and she explained it as though something had just clicked in her head **and** in her heart.

The way out of this pattern was to come back to her body and to listen to (and with) her heart, instead of listening to her head. The way out of this pattern was to step out of her self-doubt, even if that meant risking failure. With this new self-awareness, she could no longer stay stuck.

She had a new roadmap to follow; and it came from her heart. It guided her to step up and step out again by stepping into her power, by getting out of her head, and by giving herself permission to cut the cords to her overthinking.

It asked her to live and work in a way that didn't feel draining, in a way that didn't ask her to constantly prove her 'enoughness', in a way that meant she didn't have to strive, force or push.

She said to me: 'I can now see how **less is more**. I can see how I can manage feeling overwhelmed, and sustain the creation and management of the things I want to do in my business and life—the goals I want to set and reach—without burning out. I can see how I can keep going, in a sustainable, long-term way, by listening to my heart and tuning into my body's wisdom and energy.'

Yes!

When we got to the clearing and alignment part of our session, we set some goals for her, and then cleared the stress around them through kinesiology and energetic clearing. A list of some of the goals follows. You may like to use these goals as affirmations too (and if any stress comes up around these goals, do some journaling around them, or do some tapping with the Emotional Freedom Technique to clear the stress).

— Alignment goals —
— It's safe for me to take action and put myself out there
— I am energised by my work
— I am energised by taking action
— I know I'm doing enough
— I work and show up in my business and life in a sustainable way
— I flow with my energy
— I'm in tune with the energy of my business
— I am enough
— I lead from my heart
— I reconnect with my true self
— I find stillness and I slow down to reconnect
— I allow things to be easy
— I trust my enoughness

— Getting into your body —
If your mind is telling you to keep thinking, to stay in your head, to ruminate over every possible scenario (and even

scenarios that are probably not possible), then the remedy is the opposite. The opposite is to get out of your head and into your body; this is where your answers lie.

Your answers are in your body, and they're probably not the same answers (or overthinking thoughts) that you find in your mind. The answers from your body are real and grounded, not scared and worried.

So please, come back into your body now. Take a deep breath in and out. Ask your body and your heart what it needs, what it's trying to tell you. And then listen and trust and breathe it in. Be compassionate to yourself, but also let your chatter go.

You don't need to think more; you need to trust more.

— Tap, tap, tap —

One of the most simple and beautiful ways to get out of your head is to come back into your body. To do this, I find it's helpful to really feel your body again. I remember one morning, when I was starting to feel much more in sync with myself, my yoga teacher gave us an exercise where we stood at the top of our yoga mats and, with our eyes closed, softly and gently tapped our bodies, from our heads to our toes, with a light pat.

My entire body started tingling and I felt so alive, so grounded and so safe, exactly where I stood. My yoga studio is on the first floor of a building but I felt like I was rooted to the earth in the greatest sense possible. I felt like me; whole and sure and still and here.

Try it for yourself. Stand up if you can, and gently pat your body, starting at the top of your head, and going all down your face and neck and shoulders and all the way down to your toes.

Breath work is also beautiful and important, and incredibly grounding. So breathe in the energy of you, and let yourself get back into your body, all the way back in, so that you feel like yourself: whole and sure and still and here.

— A rumbling of your base —

After a failure, and before your next up-levelling, it might feel as though the ground beneath your feet isn't quite there; like you're standing on something but you're not sure what it is. It doesn't feel quite like the old ground you once stood on, and you're not yet sure if this is your new ground either. It can feel scary, unsettling and uncertain.

So what do you do? Ground in it anyway; let your footprints mark your new territory. Stand there so the ground expands around you; so it knows how far to go. Stand there in your power, with your energy flowing down into the earth beneath your feet, and find a firm, new and stable foothold.

Before I really had to ground into my new base, I felt like I had such a beautiful and deep connection to my higher chakras. I felt like I was really in tune with my crown chakra (connection to universal energy and higher self), my brow chakra (vision, clarity, intuition) and—apart from my experience during the sound healing evening—with my throat chakra too (freedom of expression, self-truth, inner truth).

As a result of my challenge, I realised that I had to more deeply connect with and heal my heart chakra too (love, acceptance, forgiveness), my solar plexus chakra (self-confidence, personal power, will) and of course my lower two chakras: my sacral (creativity and creative confidence, fertility, balancing and integrating feminine and masculine energies) and, most importantly, my base chakra (grounding, connection, tribe).

At times, my base chakra felt so rumbly that I thought I'd be swallowed whole by it; this was—in fact—during moments of my biggest expansion. The crumbling of my old foundations around me became the building blocks of my future—my new path to follow. I just couldn't see it yet.

Your most intense moments of feeling ungrounded may come right before your biggest expansion too. The crumbling down of what you know is paving the way for what's to come; you simply can't see the new path, because the old mess hasn't settled into its new beauty yet. The old is becoming the new. So be patient, and trust. You'll see it soon.

Will you be ready to let go of your old limits, expand, integrate and up-level? Will you let the energy you stand in, the ground you stand on, become more expansive, hold you more steadily, and feel illimitable?

Of course you will. Of course you can. That's why you're here.

Affirmations for grounding your energy

I am here, now

I allow myself to ground my energy

I ground my energy with ease, love and devotion

My energy is clear, cleansed, grounded and balanced

I am grounded

I am 100 percent ready, willing and able
to clear and ground my energy

I release my overthinking, because I trust in
the wisdom and power of my body

I am rooted to Mother Earth

I am connected with my earth energy

I am earth, I am grounded, I am here now

chapter 22

THE SPACE BETWEEN DREAMS AND GOALS

There is a space between most things in life, from the simple and small (like from ordering your coffee to that first sip of bliss), to the large and complex (like setting those sweet, big goals and seeing them turn into sweet, solid reality). But there is always a space in between, and we mostly get to choose what we make of it. (I say 'mostly' because to say 'always' would mean we can control the journey and the outcome. We all know we can't, and that's a good thing.)

The space between setting your goals and seeing your dreams become reality can be sweet and slow and golden. Or it can feel rocky and uncertain, fraught with difficulty and pain, with resentment and anger, with impatience and panic. The former will come through patience and trust, surrender and aligned action. The latter will come through rushing, impatience, not trusting and not staying in your flow.

The beauty and the beast of it is that you get to choose. You have a choice. You get to decide how you want to be in those spaces in between. Mostly, it would be lovely if you aligned to being patient, but I understand that 'patient' isn't always a word we want to spell out in those moments between our dreams.

I know the feeling of wanting to race and rush from the inception of an idea to its sweet completion. A little while ago, I was feeling a bit down about something, racing ahead as I'm prone to do, because I felt so far away from the thing I wanted to make and create and receive. I said to my husband, 'I just can't see it happening'. As soon as I said that, I felt myself leaking energy; leaking precious creative energy, precious receptive energy, precious empowerment and pure possibility. I was saying 'no' to myself before I'd even begun.

Then I realised, it's not about seeing it **now**. If the thing you want to create isn't here yet, it's just not here yet. That's okay! It doesn't mean you're not still creating it, or making space to receive it, on a level you can't see yet.

Instead of feeling impatient when you can't see progress, allow yourself to feel content in the spaces in between your dreams and your goals. This is about opening to flow, trusting in divine timing, and believing it'll happen when it's meant to, if it's meant to, when you are aligned and open to letting it happen, and co-creating it too. It's about letting it go, so that what you desire (or something better) can come to you … when you're ready.

— Goals, goals, goals —

A few years ago, I received an email from a prospective client who was inquiring about my business coaching and kinesiology alignment sessions. She sounded lovely, and she'd crafted a wonderful email, explaining where she was at and where she wanted to go. However, soon after reading her email, I knew we wouldn't be a good fit. (And not just because she told me that she'd gone through several other business coaches in the past year, and none of them had helped her ... warning bells!)

She'd listed her goals in her email, and they went something like this: she wanted a fully-booked coaching schedule; she wanted to create several eCourses and digital resources that would bring in lots of passive income; she wanted to film weekly videos that would win awards; she wanted to build her business to a seven-figure level, and she wanted to do all of that (and more) within the next twelve months.

I said to myself: 'Great, she seems dedicated, driven and devoted. She has big, bold goals. Let me see where she's at online and what her engagement is like.' So I looked her up online and discovered she hadn't started coaching anyone yet, she had seven Facebook followers, an empty YouTube channel and her website wasn't even up yet.

Now, there was absolutely nothing wrong with her dreams or where she was at in her business. We all start somewhere. There was nothing wrong with her social media numbers. There was nothing wrong with anything, except that her expectations were so high in the sky, they were blinding.

There's more than a fine line between having wonderful, uplifting and empowering goals that stretch you to be your best self, while you build and grow and move towards your future, and having expectations that would require a spacecraft to launch you into something you aren't nearly ready for.

That's why the space in between your goals and your dreams exists: it's to get you ready for what's to come. If you rush this process, who's to say you'll be truly ready to receive what's about to arrive? If you rush this process, if you're so focused on the future, you may not even notice your dreams if they arrived in a different form today.

I put my thoughts into words, letting her know that of course I'd love to support and coach her, but gently explaining that her goals may take some time and that deep, true and lasting success doesn't happen overnight. (And you wouldn't even want it to.) Lo and behold, I never heard from her again.

Respect and honour your dreams, and give them time to mature. Imagine if you started school at age five and your parents were like, 'Okay great, are you ready to graduate next week? We really want to hurry this process up.' You wouldn't be ready for that. Why are your big hopes and dreams any different? What makes you think they don't also need time to evolve and grow, to develop and mature? And honestly, what is the point in rushing?

— Breaking it down activity —

If trusting in a future outcome feels too hard or far away, try this activity:

— In your journal or notebook, write down some of your big, bold, beautiful dreams and goals
— Now break each goal down into at least ten steps
— If possible, try to ensure that at least a few of those steps are possible for you to work towards, or take action on,

in the next few days and weeks (even if you won't get the full outcome, you'll feel so good taking baby steps)
— Now, go and take some action ...

This activity will help you feel as though you're creating movement and momentum, because you will be. And most importantly, it'll help you see that big dreams don't happen overnight. You might need to take a thousand little steps to make them happen, and how good will you feel while on your way, as well as when you get there?

Well, that's up to you.

— Your dreams can work, even if you don't —

You may have heard the saying: *Your dreams don't work unless you do.* Well, although I am a huge advocate of taking consistent, aligned and abundant action towards your dreams, I do think they can work, even if we don't (always) work, and so I'm calling that saying out.

I'm calling it out because, on the one hand, I believe that we need to align to our goals and dreams, take action, be resilient and resourceful and put our best effort in. But on the other hand, if you truly believe that your dreams won't work if you don't work, then what you're saying is you need to always be the one who's in control. And that is the direct and absolute opposite of being in a space of trust and surrender.

If you think you are the only one who can control your future, your destiny and your fate, you're placing a lot of pressure on yourself. And yet, how often do you think that?

So let's rewrite that story. Let's be honest—our dreams are not **just** up to us. We have free will (and plenty of it) but we cannot control our future. So I believe—with the right balance and blend of intention and desire, trust and flow, gratitude and openness—our dreams can work, even if we don't.

And that space in between is made up of surrender and trust, of receiving and manifesting, of pure intention and a devotion to our dreams.

Our dreams can work without us, because they are not only up to us.

— The middle ground —

I just got off a Skype call with a lovely client who's embarking on a new adventure in her life. She's been feeling (understandably) a little bit overwhelmed by all the 'unknowns', wondering if everything will work out. During our session we spoke about trust; and about showing up, no matter what. We realigned her towards her goals and dreams, and cleared any stress around them. Then, towards the end of our session, she said to me that the unknown of not going ahead with her goals, of not honouring her dreams, would feel worse than sitting in this known unknown—the unknown of the space just before her dreams actualise, just before her goals become reality.

This realisation of hers doesn't make the unknowns any more 'known', but it makes the space in between her dreams feel calmer, less turbulent. It helps her feel more confident in herself, in her dreams and in her actions. It helps her invite more joy into her life, and feel amore aligned with her internal wisdom.

To find contentment in the space between your goals and the reality of your dreams, you must find the middle ground. Actually, rewind that; you must **create** your middle ground. This is good news. In fact, it's great news, because the middle ground is where it feels good to make your dreams come true, without rushing or questioning or doubting yourself. The middle ground is the opposite of that mysterious and illusive 'one day.' The middle ground is where your life happens.

The middle ground you create is all of those moments where you take action, while staying in your flow. It's where you make a plan, and then tune into receptivity. It's where you balance your masculine energy of doing and acting and striving, with your feminine energy of flowing and receiving and being. It's where you release expectations of what your dreams need to look like, while still making space to allow yourself to receive them.

And guess what? Your middle ground is always changing and shifting. And rightly so, because so are you. You are not the same person you were when you created your goals (even if you only created them moments ago). So of course, the ground you stand on will look and feel and be different now, compared to then. How perfect.

— The space between dreams and goals table —

Use this table to set some beautiful (and specific, but expectation free!) goals. Make note of how you want to feel in the space in between, how you'll allow yourself to feel this way, as well as which actions you can take now to bring this goal to reality.

To help, I've given you a real life example of a goal I set during the writing of this book.

My goal/ intention	How do I want to feel in the space in between?	How can I allow myself to feel this way?	What actions can I take now?
Example: I am aligned to finishing the second draft of my book during my solo writing trip to Byron Bay	Calm, focused and on track, with lots of space to let ideas come to me	Take the pressure off myself; have a flexible writing plan; say 'no' to arrangements while in Byron; make sure I rest and exercise during the trip	Make notes of what I'd like to add to the book; pack everything I need for the trip; put an auto-reply on my email that says I'm away writing

The space between dreams and goals affirmation

I allow space in between my dreams and goals, and I easily and joyfully sit in that space of surrender and trust, of beautiful and aligned action, of receiving and manifesting, of pure intention and a devotion to my dreams.

chapter 23

IT'S OKAY TO CHANGE

*I*t's okay for your goals to change. It's okay for your ground to change. It's okay to feel the rumblings of change. It's okay for you to make a goal one day, and change it the next. It's okay for you to change your mind.

It's especially okay to change your mind after a failure. It doesn't mean you've failed 'more'. I used to think it did. I used to think if I failed, I clearly just had to try harder at the thing I'd failed at. I didn't realise I could change my mind, ask myself what else I wanted, and change direction. I thought failure meant 'try the same thing again.' I didn't realise failure gives us the freedom to try **anything** else. The 'try again' part is about getting up after a failure, but you get to choose what you do next: will you get back on your horse and try something new, or something old? There's no right or wrong; there's only what feels good, and what doesn't.

— **The dilemmas of dreaming** —

I believe we can face dilemmas in our dreams when one of two things happens: firstly, we erroneously believe we have to stick to our guns with old goals that don't fit anymore; or secondly, we erroneously think we 'should' do something, because of an internal or external pressure that's been placed on us.

Fear of changing our minds, or pressure to do something because of 'shoulds'—notice how neither of those options feels good? If we simply gave ourselves permission to change our minds, if we let go of internal and external pressures to do something a certain way, the dilemmas we think we face would fade into the background, and our deepest desires would surface.

You won't have a dilemma if you give yourself permission to do what feels good to you now, today, in this moment, and not because of some past promise you made (to yourself or someone else), when you thought the future would look different.

— Old goals that don't fit —

If an old goal doesn't fit anymore, give yourself full permission to let it go. I know it might feel hard and scary, because I've done it myself many times. I also know it feels freeing and wonderful and light, because I've done it myself many times.

As an example, a few years after I graduated as a naturopath and nutritionist, I decided I should probably do some extra study. I decided to enrol in a Master of Human Nutrition, because I was worried that my naturopathy qualification wasn't enough. (Enough for who, or what, I wasn't exactly sure at the time. Now I know it was my perception that I wasn't enough without it.)

Long story short … I applied, got in, started the first subject and I didn't enjoy it at all! Apart from the fact that the content was so similar to what I'd already studied, the essays were long and boring to write. I also realised I didn't need to be studying those public health-focused subjects, in order to further my own holistic wellness business. It was also probably not the greatest time to enrol in a post-graduate course. Nic and I had just married; we'd bought a puppy (a Japanese Spitz we named Miso); I was knee-deep in establishing my business, running it from two different clinics, working on my first eBook, running my first webinars; and to top it all off, I had also just decided to study kinesiology. Wow! (Side note: that was the year I started getting heart palpitations from stress and burnout. I wonder why?) *Facepalm*

After the first or second subject, I realised I had enrolled in this course for the wrong reasons. Yes, it felt cool to say 'I'm doing my Masters' and I felt like I was accomplishing something, but I was doing it because I thought I should. I thought people would judge me or think me underqualified if I didn't have the degree (even though my business was blooming and I had lots of lovely clients, who never asked me where I'd studied). I had it all wrong. And so, I finished enough of the Master's degree to take an early exit and attain a Graduate Certificate of Human Nutrition, and I never looked back (except to continue paying off the university fees!).

Once I'd decided that this old goal didn't fit anymore, and that I didn't want to complete the course, I didn't give myself a hard time about it. I didn't tell myself I was a quitter or a failure. I simply acknowledged and honoured this wonderful truth: I could change my mind.

And so can you.

— Where's the pressure coming from? —

If you're feeling pressured to stick with a goal that doesn't fully fit you, ask yourself where the pressure is really coming from. Take, for example, my story of studying for my Master's (or almost studying it, ha!). I thought there was external pressure, when in reality, all the pressure was coming from myself.

If I hadn't studied the course at all, or on the flip side, if I had completed it in its entirety, I'm confident I'd be in exactly the same position I'm in now (with the exception that I wouldn't be telling you this story, of course). Why? Because that Master's degree wasn't calling me on a very deep level, and it wasn't something that I needed to be doing to expand into who I am today.

It was an external goal, not a soul goal. I did it because I thought I should, not because I deeply, truly wanted to; not because I thought about it all the time; not because I felt a pull towards it; and certainly not because I'd regret not doing it. I did it because I thought I'd be more accomplished if I did. In doing so, I realised it was taking precious time away from other things that called to me—like my kinesiology study, which forms the foundation of my work to this day. Without kinesiology, I know for sure I wouldn't be where I am today; I wouldn't have the business or life I have today and I wouldn't be writing this book.

Look into today's mirror, not some looking glass from the past, and you will see the present for exactly what it is: everything that you need right now, in order to get you to where you're going. Drop the pressures, drop the 'shoulds' and the expectations, and do what feels good for you now.

Follow your heart—it really does lead you in the right direction. Feel into where you're being called and pulled to … then go there.

It's okay to change affirmation

I give myself full permission to change. It's okay for me to change my mind, my dreams, my goals and my direction. I honour where I am now, what's calling me, and where I feel myself being pulled towards. I can do what feels good for me, now.

---

chapter 24

COMPASSION PREVAILS

When I was in my early twenties, I went to a little beach town in Queensland on a family holiday. One afternoon, I decided to go into the town to get my nails done. The nail technician, a girl a few years younger than I was, proceeded to paint not just my nails, but right onto my cuticles and the surrounding skin. I looked down in horror at my nails, and she beamed right back at me. She had no idea that painting cuticles is the opposite of a 'successful' manicure, and I was too scared of upsetting her to say anything. So I walked out of the nail salon with the worst manicure ever, went home and removed it all.

I think so many of us become scared of that happening to us; of being the one who thinks she's doing so well, but in the eyes of others is not (yet). We become scared of getting caught out for not being as perfect and successful as we want everyone to think we are. We worry we are failing, every day, and that one day someone will ask us to pack our things into a cardboard box and leave the building.

But what if it had been that girl's first day at the salon? What if she had only just started her training as a nail technician? What if she'd just left a really terrible job, and was just taking a break between big life choices and helping out at her cousin's salon? What if she thought she was doing an amazing job? What if she'd just broken up with her boyfriend and wasn't concentrating? What if I'd just kindly pointed out the extra paint job that I didn't need and asked her to remove it?

It must be said that compassion (to self and others) needs to prevail through all of your inner healing and your goal setting, your resilience building and your discovery of how resourceful you truly are.

Compassion prevailing through failure and beyond looks like:

— Loving yourself, no matter what is going on around you
— Knowing you can both work towards your dreams and be content with where you stand now
— Looking within, when it feels as though you don't want to know what's really going on
— Understanding that your ego's mantra is: *More, more, more!* But your heart's mantra is: *Everything is as it needs to be, you're okay, you're enough, you're doing enough*
— Knowing you can create healthy boundaries that support you and protect your energy, and not feeling guilty for this
— Giving yourself permission to stand up again if you think you've fallen, and then more permission to stand up again, and again, and again, if you think you've fallen again, and again, and again

— Forgiving yourself (instead of holding a grudge) to help you move onwards, upwards and forwards

— Asking for a friend —

A simple (and fun) exercise I can give you, to help you see if you need to be more compassionate with yourself, is this: write a letter to a friend or someone you care deeply about, explaining what you're going through and how you're feeling. I suggest handwriting it on some gorgeous paper. In this letter, you may be as specific and raw as you desire. Get it all out—your fears and your perceived dashed hopes, and everything in between.

Now ... post it to yourself (not to your friend).

When the letter arrives, read it to yourself as if it were sent from your friend (the one you initially thought you'd be sending it to).

Where is the compassion now? It's probably streaming out of you, towards your friend. Ask yourself, if the situation were reversed and this letter had indeed come from your friend, would you ever judge them for what had been written? Most likely you wouldn't. You'd probably write them a beautiful, loving and compassionate reply, right?

If you can treat others with love and compassion, you can do the same for yourself. You don't need to pretend you're 'asking for a friend.' (I know what you're thinking ... yes, you can totally write a reply letter to yourself. I won't tell anyone that you're pen pals with yourself. It's cool, your secret's safe with me.)

Compassion affirmation

I allow myself to be kind, gentle and compassionate to myself. I know I can work towards my dreams and be happy and content with where I am today. I know I am doing enough.

A NEW YOU IS BORN THROUGH

THE FIRE OF FAILURE.

———

#itsallgoodbook

chapter 25

YOUR RIVER IS DIFFERENT NOW

Raise your standards and the
universe will meet you there.

DANIELLE LAPORTE

et's talk about up-levelling. I could talk about this all day;
it's potentially one of my favourite parts of surrendering.
And yes they're a team. (Actually, every process you'll go
through in this book is part of the bigger picture, with
everything adding up to be more powerful when put together.)

Up-levelling is a recalibration—a new 'you' is born
through the fire of failure and so an up-levelling is required.

Up-levelling is what happens after we've fallen, as we're
getting back up. It's what happens when we realise we'll
never stand where we once stood before; we have changed,
we have grown, and it's now our time to give ourselves an
energetic promotion.

Once you up-level, you can't go back. You can't unlearn
what you've learnt. You can't not feel what you've felt. You

might visit old territories again, but you'll never stake it as your land—your home—again.

Up-levelling is your invitation to step up. Will you accept it? It might be unusual, it might not be what you initially thought you wanted, but it's here. And you must believe in yourself and back yourself; you must rise to meet yourself where you are.

Up-levelling is a realisation that you are different, and your river is different. We can look behind us at the landscape we've just crossed and we can say, 'That was great, then. But this is where I stand, and what I need, now.'

— It's time to move up —

With my private client work, I can't tell you how often my weeks have a common theme—even though I'm working with clients at different stages of their businesses and lives.

In real time as I write, this week has been about up-levelling (and how divinely timed too). This week, each of my clients has woken up—awakened—to being in a certain stage of their worlds and they've realised that it's time to move up.

Before they got to this stage though, they went through a few others: visualising their dreams and goals; then resistance to them; then fear of making them happen (or allowing them to happen); then overwhelm and confusion, among other stages. Then they went through the later stages: the knowing, the trust and the flow, before finally deciding it's their time, and realising that they're ready to up-level their energy and their thoughts, their intentions and their actions.

— The layers of up-levelling —

Some of these layers might feel great to you, and some might make you feel wobbly. Often when you're called to surrender, your up-levelling has already begun on some level, so pat yourself on the back for being here already. Then get ready to make space to move higher and deeper, to awaken to your new reality with all the lessons contained, with all the callings of your soul ready for you to rise, expand and flow.

— Visualising

This is the first step in your up-levelling journey, and often we don't even realise we're taking it. This may be veiled in something like daydreaming about your future, your ideal working environment or new home, the next step in your relationship, business or personal development. Sometimes it's veiled in something less than pleasant, like feeling triggered by comparison or a feeling of panic that you're 'not quite there yet.' Either way, this is an important step, for if you haven't visualised where you're going (or where you want to go), how will you ever know when you're getting closer to it?

— Resistance

Ah, our dear friend resistance. Say hello and thanks for sharing, then be ready to do what you've come here to do anyway. This layer of up-levelling has no designated length of time; you stay here for as long as you let yourself. When you can no longer be where you sit, when you feel more than ready to leap, jump and step up, you'll leave this stickiness of resistance and step into a higher vibration. You might not always feel completely ready, but staying will feel worse (or less than best, or not enough, like you know you're capable of more) than leaving and moving on up. It's time for more depth, more breadth, and more space for you. Are you ready? Feel the resistance and do it anyway. Say 'yes' then step up.

— Fear

Once you've passed through resistance, fear can pop up. It might not even feel all that different from resistance, except that it's stronger or clearer. Resistance can feel foggy; it's those slight, tiny, small sensations, like little invisible cobwebs that hold you back and you can't quite put your finger on them. Fear is stronger; it feels like you're being gripped within your heart and held back for your own safety. But truly, you are safe stepping up too. You are what is safe, so go with yourself to your next level and leave the fear behind. Or do what I do: feel the fear and say, 'Thanks for sharing.' Then, do what you came here to do anyway.

— Letting go and simplifying

Clearing and making space might be very physical (cupboard clean-outs, washing your car etc.), but it can also pop up in other areas of your life that don't always feel as simple. You might find that you simplify things like eating, exercise or home life, so you're more able to easily invest in other areas like up-levelling your energy, focusing on your intentions, and bringing your new dreams to life. Let go, make space for yourself—your softest, most real self—to show up. When you up-level, there will always be something for you to let go of, so that you can step up. So, what is it?

— Overwhelm and confusion

Okay, now you've looked your dreams, your resistance and your fear in the eyes and in the heart. Now you're wondering: 'Um, okay, now what? Where do I start?' Start simply. Start with what feels right and true for you. Often this is after the unravelling, the rumbling, the ground breaking and crumbling and shattering beneath your feet, and so maybe where you start—and how you clear overwhelm and confusion—isn't as important as simply starting again. Take one step and then another. Start simply. But start.

— Knowing

There's a quote from A Course in Miracles that I love: *Those who are certain of the outcome can afford to wait, and wait without anxiety.* To me this means: what is the knowing that you already know? What is it that you already feel within you will come true, even if it looks different to how you imagined it, even if you don't know when it'll happen? For instance, a 'knowing' I had was that the lessons I went through during and after my failure—even though they felt so tough and challenging—would one day form the basis of my work, in some form. The form is this book. So what can you know, from a space of trust and expansion, while also letting the 'or something better' thought simmer below the surface?

— Aligning

Aligning our energy and uplifting our thoughts is a key component to living a life of surrender, resilience and trust. This calls for you to continually course-correct on your journey through surrendering to where you are, in order to move towards where you want to be, while staying in complete and beautiful integrity with who you are, and what you desire.

— Root to rise

There's something my yoga teachers often say in class: 'Root to rise.' They say this when they want us to feel grounded as we rise up into a pose, so that we don't lose our footing, so that we are strong in our flow, rooted yet full of fluidity and movement. Root to rise means to become grounded in where you stand, so you can rise higher (and higher, and higher). It asks you to be really sure of where you stand, to be focused on where you stand, and to be really centred in that space, so that you have the energy and the integrity to move into where you want to be.

Recalibrating after you've been shaken up is about you grounding your energy, to come back to yourself in a new light. Recalibrating is a gift. You've already been shown what is out of alignment, what needs to go, what needs to arrive— or what's already rushing in to fill its place—and you're seeing a glimpse of your new land. This land, this ground, this earth is where you stand now. So let yourself root into the ground, into Mother Earth, into nature, into your new and natural path of rising and … let yourself recalibrate. Your energy needs this new space, and you are worthy of it.

— Leaving, so you can arrive —

When you up-level your energy, your thoughts, and your mindset, you sometimes leave others behind. This is okay.

It's not your job to help carry others; we must each take this journey ourselves.

During my months of initiation into a new way of being, and of clearing guilt, grief, regret and disappointment, some of my friendships changed. Some deepened, new ones formed, and I let some old ones go.

Sometimes this was on my part. A friendship that feels draining and depleting, that pushes boundaries and leaves you feeling resentful, is not supportive of you up-levelling your energy. But I also experienced the loss of a friendship that hadn't felt depleting—in fact, I had loved that friendship, and felt we were so close for so long. But during this period, it became clear that on some level, our energies were no longer aligned. When I could see the friendship changing and dissolving, I tried to put more attention, love and care into it. But it became clear to me that this wasn't being reciprocated, and that it was time to let it go.

While the ending of that friendship initially felt quite hard to take, and I definitely mourned the loss of it, I could also see that forcing it to stick wasn't going to work. I didn't understand why it had happened, but that didn't mean I couldn't accept it. *Flow, not force* became my new mantra. I really did let myself grieve the end of that friendship in its previous form; I also trusted that if we were meant to cross paths again, that it would happen in its own time. I didn't want to hold onto things (friendships or otherwise) that felt hard. So again, I was reminded that I had to surrender and let go to move to my next level.

Up-levelling affirmation

I allow myself to start with what feels good and right and true for me. I let go, I ground myself in my new energy, and I make space for myself to show up, and to rise up. I am ready to up-level my energy, and I am ready for the next step.

chapter 26

THE PATH OF ASCENSION

As I write this, I've just finished a kinesiology align-ment session via Skype, with a client who is deeply and beautifully aware of her intuition. The timing of our session—on the day I'd planned to expand this exact chapter—couldn't have been more perfect (of course). The session was all about growth, change, integration, up-level-ling, finding new ground and trusting that, even if you feel a little blind to your path, you're heading in the right direction.

My client told me that she had been feeling disconnected lately. For a long time, she'd been feeling so in tune on a mental, emotional and spiritual level. But recently she had spent more time and energy connecting to her body on a physical level, learning how to listen to and trust her body. Now she felt as though she'd lost connection to her mental, emotional and spiritual self.

She asked me, 'Why don't I feel amazing, if I'm more connected to my body now, and listening to my body more?' I suggested that maybe she was in an integration phase;

integrating the changes in her physical awareness, to feel even more integrated throughout her mental, emotional, physical and spiritual bodies.

We spoke about this for a little while, then she paused, took a breath and said, 'I'm realising that on the path of ascension, I might face a challenge, then I'll level up, then I'll face another challenge, then level up ... it's a process. So what I'm in right now is a levelling-up too.'

Yes! Being in the space between a challenge and an up-level is new ground, and you may not have stood there before, and you may never stand there again. You will rise up, again and again. You will level up, again and again. And you can trust this process; trust that you won't feel blind for long; trust that *this too shall pass*; trust the next level of trust. You can trust that even if you're feeling wobbly now, it's okay to feel different on every level. Even if this level feels like it drags on, even if you could feel the change, but not yet see the outcome. From the moment it started, even if your future vision has gone foggy, you, like my client, will survive it and feel all the better for it.

These are the goals we aligned her to. You make like to work with them too:
— It's safe for me to change
— I love and accept myself
— I align, integrate and connect my four bodies
— I evolve my connection to myself on all levels
— I allow myself to go deeper with my connection to myself
— I trust my body in its cyclic nature and wisdom
— I open up to the energies of ease, trust and wisdom

As soon as our session was over, she sent me a message saying she'd been feeling so down that morning, but now felt so refreshed, clear and amazing.

Yes, energy had shifted through our session. But even more than that, the rush of clear, refreshed energy was thanks to her permission to allow herself to be in the space of not knowing; to trust that integration was happening and that her up-level was only a matter of time; and to stay in a space of trust, trust and more trust ... trusting that her connection to herself was always evolving, ever-deepening, and so very perfect exactly as it was.

— Greater heights —

In upgrading your energy, you will find new ground on which to stand, and new footing to help you climb to even greater heights. You may also be tested on where you stand—is this the new energy you really want to embody? Is this really where you want to stand? Are you very sure this is where you want to direct your energy? These are the kinds of questions you might find yourself bumping up against on your way to (your own version of) the top. Embrace them, relish them, then answer them through your intentions, your grace and your desire to keep expanding into who you are.

For me, a huge part of my recalibration into the energy I wanted to embody in myself, and extend into the world, came down to up-levelling. Up-levelling my thoughts, up-levelling my actions, up-levelling my energy. When we up-level, we also integrate. When we integrate, we also recalibrate. When we recalibrate, we are ready to face the world as a higher, brighter, deeper and more grounded version of ourselves.

— Up-levelling your energy isn't just about you —

Up-levelling your energy helps the people around you too. When you become clear on how you've grown and where you're going (and growing to), then you can help others get there too, by showing them what's possible.

Of course, as you may have witnessed yourself, you can't surrender for someone else, but you can hug them and buy them flowers or tea or a rose quartz crystal, and let them know that everything will be okay too. Who could up-level alongside you, if you up-level now?

New ground affirmations

These energy-balancing affirmations will help you shift old energy and make space for the new, so that you can stand strong atop the new ground you've created for yourself:

It's my time, and I am ready to step up, and to step out

I am 100 percent ready, willing and able to up-level my energy

I give myself permission to up-level my energy

*I am grounded in the now, in my truth,
and in my personal power*

I am ready to move on

I am grateful to be expanding

I am 100 percent ready, willing and able to expand

I am expanding now

I trust in my expansion

I trust in my growth

I trust in where I'm going

I am ready to rise

chapter 27

TURN THE LIGHTS ON

When I started to feel myself coming out of that period in my life where I felt small, where my actions felt inconsequential and my goals and desires felt insignificant, I started to focus my energy into my visibility. When I say visibility, I don't just mean that I wanted to be seen in a business sense, and to trust that it was safe for me to be seen by a wider network, on a bigger level. I also wanted to witness myself; I wanted to be okay with looking my story in the eyes, with accepting it, and with knowing that because I'd been through it and come through the other side, my light—my visibility—was even brighter now.

For over a year beforehand, I had spent so many days walking around feeling as though I was wearing Harry Potter's invisibility cloak. I would try to speak up and hear nothing in return; I would attempt to open doors that felt wedged shut; I would try to peek into new worlds through windows into new worlds that would slam down on my fingers; and I would try to open myself up to the world in a way that showed love, devotion and commitment, only to feel too small, too inconsequential and too insignificant.

This was all—as we've gone through in previous chapters—my perception. And yet I took it as a truth; and so, for a while, it became my truth.

— You don't need to feel invisible for long —

I think I felt invisible for so long because I was still healing and integrating all my lessons. Consciously, I wanted to be 'out there' more, but I was hurting because I had put too much emphasis on my perceived failings. I was stuck in the past, thinking and wondering and worrying about what I'd done wrong. I can bounce back from many things quite quickly, but for some reason—I think because I resisted surrendering to where I was for so long—this experience took its time to take me through it.

I don't think there's anything wrong with feeling the need to hide for a little while you heal, but there'll come a time when you're ready to be visible again. There'll be a time when a surge of energy pulses through you and asks you to turn the lights on, to turn up the brightness, to shine, and to trust that you are worthy of being seen.

The difference for you to discern is whether you don't feel ready because you aren't ready yet, or whether you don't feel ready to be seen because being seen feels scary.

You might feel overwhelmed or intimidated at the thought of becoming visible again after a failure, and that is okay. We all need you to try again, though. We all need you to rise.

— Trust that it's safe to be seen —

As a result of surrendering to where I was, I found myself flowing to where I wanted to be. It was, in fact, an even better place to be, because I wasn't controlling it. (For a recovering perfectionist to say that, you know it must be real!)

I started to feel so much more visible in such a wonderful way. I would show up with pure intention and a keen curiosity, and instead of being met with disappointment (as I felt like I was getting so used to), I would find myself buoyed up by hope, by the abundance I was acknowledging and receiving, and by the sweet power and energy of reciprocity.

However, there was also a time, within weeks of feeling this lightness return to my step, my energy and my thoughts, where I noticed ways in which I felt I was being tested by my new visibility—ways that made me think I needed to do some more mindset shifting, clearing and energy balancing.

This happened in small ways that indicated some kind of misalignment: potential new clients emailing and asking for in-person sessions when I only offer online sessions; receiving lots of 'cold-calling' marketing emails; requests for online summits that didn't really fit; and other situations that made me pause, like an encounter with an online troll.

On one hand, I was so grateful to be visible to more people, but on the other hand, I realised I had to tidy up my boundaries and intentions even more, so that I became more and more visible to the right people (for me, that is).

With every surge of up-levelling, one is asked to redefine their own terms and boundaries. So once you up-level your visibility, you must create new boundaries on your new turf.

The way I did this was to reaffirm what felt right for me, through my thoughts, intentions and actions. If a prospective client emailed asking about an in-person session, I let them know that I only offer online sessions, and directed them to where they could book in if they chose to. If someone emailed me to take part in their online summit but it didn't feel right, I would simply say 'thanks, but no thanks.' If a troll left me an unkind comment, I didn't reply to them, but nor did I hide because of them. I continued to show up, to take action in a way that felt right for me and that honoured my boundaries, and to set intentions with self-compassion and devotion.

Your boundaries don't have to shift or disappear when you come back from a failure; you don't have to change the essence of who you are to fit a new mould. Be yourself, align to what works for you, and keep showing up. The right people will notice you, and even if less than right people do, that's okay. You can shine, be visible, be seen and do your own thing anyway.

Being seen affirmation

Being seen is safe for me. I trust I will allow myself to be seen when I am ready, and I trust I'll know when I am ready. I show up for myself. I have clear and healthy boundaries, and I am ready to shine.

chapter 28

THE PILOT AND THE JELLY

A while ago, I went through a period of feeling really nervous during turbulence while flying. I would grip Nic's hand, shut my eyes and try to take deep breaths until we'd flown out of the turbulence.

I was speaking to a friend about this, and she told me that she'd once had a conversation with a pilot about turbulence. He'd explained it like this: imagine you have some fruit set in a cup of jelly. Now imagine you shake the cup. The fruit will shake and wobble, but it won't drop; there's nowhere for it to fall. That's what turbulence is. It feels wobbly and shaky, but you can trust that you won't actually drop; you won't fall because of some turbulence.

With this in mind, my fear of turbulence dissipated. In its place, trust arose.

— **Trusting** —

Trusting is not always easy, but its very nature ushers in more ease. Even writing this book was a gentle reminder to trust;

to trust the flow of words that came through as I sat down to write, the timing of my life (and this book), to trust myself, and to stay steeped in trust and surrender.

I wrote the first half of this book very slowly, over almost a year. I finished the rest of the first draft very quickly in a nine-day period, and then completed the second draft in a seven-day period. But there were days, weeks and months when I didn't write a word. I had to relinquish control of my idea of when the time would be right to write, surrendering to the path of least resistance, letting go of expectations and leaning completely into trust.

So while this whole book is essentially about trust, I've come to understand that I can't make you understand trust the way I feel and understand it. I really believe we all have our own version of it. So this is what I feel it is, and I invite you to stay open to crafting your own version. After all, you'll be the one carrying yourself forward in life, with trust, in flow, and always with self-compassion. So, here we go.

To me, trust is about trusting yourself, your path in life, your decisions and actions, your support team and your value. It's about knowing that when you're going through hard moments, days, weeks or months, you'll be okay in the end. It's about staying with it all, through the tough times, knowing you're strong enough, resilient enough, resourceful enough and brave enough to make it through to the other side. Change will come, and you are strong enough to flow with it, through it and alongside it; you are strong enough to flow without resisting it, and to trust it'll take you where you need to be.

While I'm not obsessive, I am someone who likes things to be quite neat and definitely organised (I love being organised!). So the idea of leaning into uncertainty used to feel terrifying but also foolhardy. I thought that instead of letting go, I must try to think everything through a million times over. I thought that to overthink—which by (irrational) definition must mean I could control the outcome, right?— would be much better.

It wasn't. It isn't. It doesn't help.

To lean into trust is to let go of overthinking, comparison and the fear of the uncertain. It's to have self-compassion for yourself through every stage of your journey; to trust yourself to support and lift you up; and to trust your support team (the angelic, the spiritual, the human and also the chocolate kind).

To lean into trust is to know that if you can't see the answer to your problem yet, you just don't need the answer yet.

When you trust yourself enough to trust where you are right now, it helps you to see the situation clearly; you let go of the stories you're telling yourself, and you see the situation for what it is. No attachments, no ifs, shoulds or buts. You see clearly and in a calm, uncharged way.

When you trust, deeply and fully, you'll naturally feel more grounded and more powerful—not just in who you are, but in where you're going. You won't need to feel reactive, or overreact, or jump to conclusions. You won't need to 'prepare' yourself for the worst, because you trust that you are resilient enough to manage yourself in all situations, and that you are supported.

And when the time is right, the conclusion will flow to you as effortlessly as if it was always meant to, because it was meant to; and you'll see that putting more frenetically-charged energy into a situation doesn't help it play out in a better way. As my friend so wisely said, 'When you overthink something, the only one who suffers is you.'

If you can't understand how the situation will play out yet, you just don't need to know how it'll play out yet. So, in the spaces in between … trust.

If you can't understand why it's happening yet, you just don't need to know why it's happening yet. Trust you'll see the bigger picture when you're ready to.

Trust that when you need to know, see and understand, you will. All in good time … and not a moment sooner.

— It's time —

It's time to really start trusting yourself now, in order to try again, whether that means you start to explore new goals you'd like to set, or reaffirm old goals that still feel golden to you. To trust is to believe that letting go of your perceived need to control is in your best interests.

And as we've just covered, it's about trusting you can make the right decisions during future challenges—without zooming ahead and trying to work out what those might be—by trusting yourself, your intuition, inner guide and inner wisdom, your higher self and of course, the universe.

Answer this: *What would have felt different in your journey up until now, if you'd trusted that everything would be okay?* Trusting isn't about attaching to an outcome. Trusting is making aligned, peaceful and grounded decisions, whether or not we know how things will turn out (because we don't know, we can't know, and because 'knowing' would dilute our free will).

Consider these questions:

— *Think of a situation you might be worrying about. What would you want to happen for everything to feel okay for you?* Now trust the situation, exactly as it is; trust you are supported, trust you can manage it, trust yourself, the universe and your guidance, wisdom and support system enough to lean into the uncertainty of it all. It's all good; you'll be okay.

— *What are some of the steps you can take today to help you feel more empowered and grounded, to help you feel closer to your desired outcome (or something better)?*

— *If you trusted that the outcome of this situation would serve and support your highest good, how would you feel?* Excellent, now lean into that. Trust, trust, trust.

— Transcending discomfort —

There can be a discomfort associated with stepping into trust. It's like the 'fake forgiveness' we spoke about a little while ago; it's conditional on things going well. For instance, you might feel such discomfort at the thought of trusting, and then of things still not going well, that you decide to test the universe: 'Okay, so you want me to trust you again? So here's a situation that I feel worried about—let's see what you do with that!'

Um, no. This doesn't work. This is keeping you stuck in fear and it's a pretend trust. In fact, it's not really trust at all, is it? It's a feeling of resentment and bitterness, and I understand you might just be testing the waters (because I did this too, when I was stuck in fear about trusting my future).

To trust is to release bitterness and resentment and to step back into the flow of your life, knowing you're already strong enough to handle what is flowing to you, and what you are drawing inwards.

— Releasing illusions —

With my desire and commitment to up-level my thoughts, energy and mindset came something else: the desire and drive to replace my illusions of what had happened in relation to my failure with a deep sense of trust. This deep trust would support me in believing that I would know how to navigate my future with more ease, more grace, and even more trust. (Yes, learning how to trust that you can trust yourself is part of this process too.)

I was scared of making the same mistakes again, but I also knew that, if a similar situation were to present itself, I would now have new skills, a deeper knowledge, and more resilience and resourcefulness to handle it all beautifully.

There's the trusting of your future, but there's also the trusting that you'll know how to meet your future, how to act intentionally in your future, and how to let go of the fear of making the same mistakes again. Trusting that you'll be able to manage yourself well in the future, when difficulties arise, is part of your surrendering, up-levelling and recalibrating process.

I soon realised that my fear of making the same mistakes was an illusion. It wasn't real; it was the fear of a future fear that hadn't even emerged yet—the fear of fear itself—and it was suffocating me, stifling my progress and my growth, and keeping me stuck.

To let it go, I had to ground myself in the present moment, point out all I'd learnt through this process, and remind myself that I could trust myself to make the right choices and decisions.

To let it go meant I could get on with taking action again, trusting that even if I failed again, I would still be okay. Now it's time for you to do the same thing too.

Trust affirmations

These affirmations will help you ground your energy and release your fears and illusions, so you can trust in yourself, and your path in life:

I allow myself to trust, opening up to the energies of flow, trust and surrender

I allow life to support me

I trust myself, my guidance and my intuition

I trust myself, my choices, actions and decisions

I trust my path in life

I trust the timing of my life

I tune into trust and let go of what I no longer need, knowing it is safe for me to do this

I know I am capable of trusting myself

I am 100 percent ready, willing and able to trust myself

I believe in myself

It's safe for me to see clearly

I know how to see clearly and take action from a calm, grounded space

I know I am strong and resilient enough to handle all situations beautifully

Moving on now (again).

chapter 29

YOU ARE SAFE

———

Several months into my healing from failure, I sometimes found myself feeling panicky about money. I only had to think about my bank account for tears to spring to my eyes; my chest would feel heavy, as if there were bricks on it; my throat would feel like it was closing up.

I've mentioned the lung stuff that I went through—processing and healing from guilt, grief and regret—but this was something different.

Because of all the money I'd invested in my big project, and even though over the next year I slowly made it all back, there were times where it felt like I just didn't have enough. This was a feeling of pure panic around money and financial security: panic that I wouldn't have enough, that I didn't have enough, that I'd never have enough, and that even if I could have enough, I'd block myself from receiving it or manage it poorly and spend it all. I walked around with this sense of lack and loss, and it was exhausting.

I still had quite a few outgoing business expenses related to my big project at the time, and the thought of them sometimes overwhelmed me. I remember a week when I hadn't been able to pay myself a salary from my business, because of all the expenses. When I checked my personal bank balance, it was $18 in deficit. It was only $18, and I could transfer some money from a savings account to get back in the black until I could pay myself a salary again but, oh my goodness, did I feel like a failure!

There were two occasions where this feeling of not having enough manifested in panic attacks. I knew what was happening, because I've worked with clients who've had panic attacks, so while it obviously wasn't a pleasant experience, the actual panic attack didn't frighten me. But it very meaningfully showed me that my mind and body weren't coping well with my financial fears.

In a bizarre way, the physical manifestations of my panic attacks—the actual panic attack, the hyperventilating and such—almost felt like a physical release of the mental and emotional energy I'd been holding onto in relation to these fears. So while I was there in a panic attack, part of my brain was saying: 'Calm down Cass. It's okay. You're just having a panic attack,' and the other part was saying: 'This kind of feels good, this is a release. This is my body showing me what I need. I needed this.'

I know that might sound a bit odd, especially to people who've experienced panic attacks, and I don't mean to offend anyone who has them and has had a very different experience to me. I think I had this experience because I know what a panic attack looks like, so when it happened to me, I could see it for exactly what it was. I knew that even though I was reacting on a physical level, I was still safe. I also had both panic attacks at home, in a space where I do feel safe, and I'm sure this helped on some level too.

I started to take extra steps to clear, ground and calm my energy through energetic clearing, kinesiology, money mindset work, meditation, herbal medicines, energetic essences, good food, and sleep. I also made sure to keep up with my daily movement and exercise.

I knew that one of the best things to do during a panic attack is to move your body. This really worked for me. Staying in a crouched position and hyperventilating can keep you there for longer than necessary, whereas getting up, walking, doing some jumping jacks or moving around helps to 'switch off' the panic mode, the fight or flight response. It helps you get back into your body, and helps your body get back into you. It reminds you that you are okay, you are here, and you are safe.

— Do you have enough for today? —

Around this time, I remember speaking to my parents about my financial worries and my dad said to me, 'Do you have enough money for today, for right now?' He was asking me this to help me come back into the present moment. And the answer was always 'Yes, just enough' or 'Yes, barely.' But I did have enough for today. I might not have had enough for next week, or next month, or next year … but I had enough for today. And every subsequent time I asked myself that question (even if it happened to be in the period of 'next week' that had seemed so stressful the week before), I found I could answer: 'Yes, I have enough for today.'

— See the enoughness —

I was so terrified of not having enough, but it was always future tripping, with me saying to myself: 'I won't have enough for later. I won't have enough in the future.'

During this period, a beautiful friend of mine invited me to think about receiving money as opening the doorway of money to me; and even if I didn't feel I had enough, to trust that more was flowing because this doorway was open.

When I could see that I had enough for right now, for today, I could see that I was okay, even if I didn't consciously think it was enough. I could trust that I was okay. This helped me see that having enough today **is** enough. That what I was building today would support me tomorrow, and from this, I could start to not only trust the money in my account, I could also trust that more money was flowing to me, even if I couldn't see it yet.

This vibration of enoughness opened the doorway for even more money to flow to me, in expected and unexpected ways. Sometimes this was through clients booking in, through online sales, through live rounds of my eCourses, through speaking gigs, events and other income streams. But sometimes it was from people in my life: going out for breakfast with a friend and my friend picking up the bill, just because; my barista making me a large coffee when I ordered a regular; or finding money on the street (just yesterday, while I was thinking about writing this chapter, I was walking to my car and found a very squished fifty cent coin on the road). Sometimes it was from my family: my hubby taking over paying some of the bigger household bills; and simply going to my parents' house for dinner and going home with leftovers, so I didn't have to think about buying or making lunch next day.

For a while, I felt guilty for receiving money (or free things) that I hadn't worked for. I would feel bad that a friend bought me breakfast, and that the barista gave me a large coffee instead of the regular one I paid for. I would feel guilty that I couldn't contribute to the household bills the way I wanted to. (I didn't feel that guilty for taking leftovers from my parents, because my dad is such a good cook ... but sometimes I felt guilty when I forgot to give the Tupperware containers back!)

You can just imagine how this extra self-flagellation helped my lungs heal, and how it helped my panic attacks ... it didn't!

I had to come back into my own sense of self-worth. I had to see that if this money (or free things like gifts, coffee or food) was flowing to me, it didn't matter from who, where, why or what. It was coming to me, and I was worthy of accepting it. I could be grateful for all the money my business was bringing in, I could take my friend out for breakfast next time, I could thank my barista, I could be deeply grateful for the money I found on the street, I could be so thankful to my hubby and contribute to the weekly food shop and household bills as much as I could, and I could cook for my parents in return.

I could see the enoughness in what I was receiving, and this in turn meant I could see I was receiving enough ... and more.

To do that though, first I had to own my worth, detach it from my idea of external success, hold it close and trust that I did indeed have enough, that I was supported, that I would be okay.

And when I look back on this period now, when I look at the actual figures from my business, I can see that while I may have made less than in previous years, I still made enough. I still opened up to receive money, and allowed myself to receive it. My fears were all in my head. When I could come back fully into my body, into trust, into abundance, I could see that I was really supported and then, in turn, receive this support with love and gratitude.

— Track it —

Another thing I began doing to acknowledge the abundance I was receiving was to track my money. Not just the physical money that came into my life, but I also tracked the value of the free gifts, food or coffee I received, even down to the five cent coins I sometimes found on the streets.

That way, I could look back and see that I was allowing myself to receive on many levels, and that I was already abundant. It was truly powerful, and something I continue to do to this day.

— Stay in abundance —

One beautiful way to tune into trust is to notice the signs and symbols of trust and support that are already all around you. Start to notice when things like feathers, coins, random signs on the street or in shop windows, or other signs of trust (such as seeing recurring numbers) start to pop up for you.

You might find yourself having a day where you're worrying about money or feeling less than abundant, and then your friend buys you lunch, or the best parking spot ever is available, or a dress you've been eyeing off is on sale, or the grocer gives you a free apple with your weekly shop, or a colleague at work unexpectedly brings you a coffee, or you find a $2 coin on the street.

Don't just ignore these hints and tastes and signs of abundance. Don't just step over the money on the street (even if it's just a five cent coin!). Pick it up and be grateful for the abundance and support you're receiving, make a mental note of it or track it, be grateful for it and allow it to be a sign that you are supported by something greater than yourself. If you start to look for these signs, you might notice they're already all around you.

— Ask for help —

If you ever find yourself feeling anxious or panicked about not having enough, or indeed just feeling anxious in general, there are many beautiful herbs that can support you through anxiety and calm your nervous system. I mentioned some of these earlier in the book (Chapter 15), but in case you need a gentle reminder, some of them are: Passionflower, Valerian, Vervain, Zizyphus, Lemon Balm, Chamomile, Motherwort, Withania and American Ginseng.

Of course, sometimes you need extra support in the form of a psychologist, a doctor, or another professional, and perhaps western medication. This is perfect too; there's no need to feel ashamed of asking for or needing help. I saw my own healer, my acupuncturist and my psychologist a few times after my panic attacks, and it all helped greatly. Please let yourself ask for help, and then receive it. There are so many people who can help you, if you only ask.

You may also like to talk about what you're going through with your friends, partner, family and colleagues. I found increasing my self-care through eating really good, nourishing foods, going to yoga, booking in a massage, making fewer arrangements on the weekends, and having less on my plate also helped me feel calmer and more grounded. And of course, keeping a chunk of the beautiful crystal, citrine, nearby is always a lovely reminder to keep you tuned into an abundance mindset.

I also saw a financial planner around this time. I was so nervous about making the appointment. I thought he would judge me and I felt so ashamed about my financial situation, that I almost cancelled the meeting. But when I was sitting there, with my Xero spreadsheets and reports all laid out, sipping on a peppermint tea and looking up at him nervously to see what he was going to say, I realised that being brave enough to look this situation in the eye—and in the heart—was how I'd heal from it more fully.

I was surprised and relieved to hear him tell me how well he thought I was doing. He pointed out things that I had brushed over, things I wasn't giving myself credit for, things that I took for granted. I left the meeting feeling so empowered, and so proud of myself. That was a healing experience in and of itself.

Abundance affirmations

Place your hands over your heart, take some deep breaths in, and then use these affirmations to tune into abundance and trust:

I tune into the energies of abundance

I acknowledge the abundance in my life

I trust in the cycle of abundance

I know I am supported

I trust I am always supported

I allow money to flow to me, and I receive it with gratitude

I trust I can receive and hold money beautifully

Money is flowing in my direction

I allow myself to receive

It is safe for me to receive

I am safe

chapter 30

IT'S THE GLUE THAT KEEPS YOU TOGETHER

---

*N*ow that you've started this process of recalibrating, of trusting, of being present in staying in the flow, how do you open yourself up in order to receive—be that trust, guidance, information, abundance or something else, or all of the above?

In order to receive, we must be clear and aligned, so this chapter is a gentle reminder that self-care and grounding are so important in order to receive. I find that out of all of these processes, opening ourselves up to receive wonderful things into our lives again, after what feels like a fall, can actually be one of the simplest. After all, it's mostly an intention, a feeling, an energy, a vibration … you've been making so much beautiful space and letting go of so much you no longer need over the past pages, so you are now ready to receive! Right? Right.

— The proverbial cup —

When we talk about self-care, we often talk about the prover-bial cup and how we must fill our own before we can give to others. This is true, of course, but imagine for a moment that your cup is too full and that you have no space in it to receive? This is how I felt for so long during my months of healing from failure. It felt as though I was 'doing' so many of the right things, yet not receiving what I desired in return.

I can see now that I was 'filling my cup' with things I didn't need: not forgiving myself, being hard on myself, being unkind to myself, rehashing the past and trying to work out what I could have done differently (to the point where I'd sometimes brainstorm what I could have done differently in a notebook, the way I'd brainstorm a new project!).

My cup was so full—overflowing, in fact—but not with things that lit me up. I had to empty my cup first, to refill it in a way that felt good to me. This emptying is part of the recalibration process—part of your up-levelling, part of your surrendering, and most definitely part of increasing your resilience and rising from a fall.

So while we've worked on forgiveness and letting go, let's spend a few moments now going deeper, down or up or across another layer, to ask: 'What am I still filling my cup with that I can let go of now?'

I'm gently prodding you to do this because, as I've mentioned before, a deep sense of failure comes with many layers of other emotions, and what I found to be so true for me was that letting go of them once wasn't always enough. So let yourself see all your layers and peel them back to forgive yourself and let some old things go (again and again and again, if necessary).

Try emptying your cup by journalling about the following prompts:

My cup is too full of …
I need to empty my cup because …
This is what's lighting me up lately; this is what I'll fill my cup with …

— Receiving is a state of being —

This is where adjusting course so you can tune into feminine flow (no matter your gender!) is the key. As we've just discussed, we have to make space in order to receive. Being in flow, working with our feminine energies, gives us that space.

So much of our experience of working out how we can surrender to where we are, so we can flow to where we want to go, is about letting go of the unhealthy version of our masculine energy—that 'constant action' way of doing things.

That mentality and too much of that energy can get us stuck in the egotistic way of thinking that tries to say: 'You're not done yet. There's still so much more to do, and you better not stop until you've done it all. And even when you've done it all, make sure you do more anyway.'

It's egotistic, because it means we think we are the only ones creating our future. But to receive and manifest in a true way is to realise, remember and embody this fact: we are co-creating our future, our destiny and our fate—it is free will mixed with synchronicity and divinity, and it's not just up to us. So let go of what you're holding onto, to make space for what you want to receive. It doesn't need to be simpler or more complicated than that.

— A drawing in —

To allow yourself to receive is to unbind yourself from the chains of expectations and presumption, in order to draw in what you **want** on a conscious level, and what you **need** on a subconscious level.

What you consciously desire is—of course—easier to discern, because it's probably something you think about often. But what about the subconscious desires? Sometimes our body and our spirit needs something that our conscious mind rebels against.

During the period where I was fighting to surrender and finding it so hard to forgive myself, my business actually slowed down, and not because I wanted it to. I saw less clients than I had in many years, and not for lack of conscious trying. However, it also felt like I didn't have the energy to keep putting into my business, because the truth is I needed the energy to heal. This was another layer of my 'failure as progression' lesson, and I think I initially found it hard to accept because it wasn't something that felt tangible or easy to explain; it was pure energy.

My energy was being contained and reserved for my healing process, and I didn't have enough to share with the same number of clients I used to see. While on some level I knew it was all energetic, I still found myself fighting against it. This happened for weeks on end, until I let it go towards the end of the year.

I realised I was actually, deeply craving my feminine self. I wanted to be okay with doing less—I mean really doing less—not just the practical, day-to-day stuff, but on an energetic level. I wanted to give myself permission to put less out there, in order to conserve more energy and flow, and receive more energy and flow. I said to myself: 'If I keep fighting this, I will keep fighting this. If I flow with this, I will flow with this.'

It sounds almost too simple to work, but that's the beauty of the feminine: it's not about work. It's not about striving, or the daily grind, or the hustle. It's also not about the perceived opposite of those words: laziness, idleness, failure.

Feminine flow is in those spaces in between. To me, it's even more than the yin to the yang—it's the yin around the yang too; it's the glue that keeps you together. I felt like I became unstuck because, in truth, I wasn't gluing myself together by being in flow, by trusting, by surrendering to where I was. I was acting on the false assumption that tuning into my feminine energy was letting go of what carried me forward—until I realised, deeply and completely, that tuning into my feminine energy **is** what carries me forwards. It's what carries you forwards too.

The receiving affirmation

I balance, clear and align my energy in order to do
so. I flow with my feminine energy. I allow myself to
receive. I receive with thanks. I receive with love.

TUNING INTO FLOW IS

WHERE THE MAGIC IS,

AND IT'S WITHIN

YOUR REACH.

#itsallgoodbook

part 3

THE BEGINNING

AND NOW YOU DREAM AND FLOW AND RECEIVE

---

chapter 31

THE CURRENT OF YOUR LIFE

*If you are irritated by every rub,
how will you be polished?*

RUMI

One of the best parts of surrendering is seeing how it then opens us up to experience flow, with a new-found appreciation of its power and grace. Tuning into the power of true flow is powerful; it's where synchronicity lives, where alignment breathes and where ease is part of your everyday life.

Tuning into flow helps us to become even more crystal clear on what it is we really want (without attaching to an outcome). It helps us live—and stay—in alignment, and in our integrity, even if it feels like things are crumbling down around us.

Tuning into flow is where the magic is, and it's within your reach.

Tuning into the natural ebbs and flows of your life is also part of staying in the energy of flow. Some days you'll feel like a river, flowing beautifully to where you want to be; some days you might feel like a stone, a little bit stuck, a little unmoving, a little heavy. But what if that was okay?

What if—instead of fighting against the flow—you just let go and went with it? If you surrender to the days when you feel heavy and stuck, those feelings will sink faster, and the lightness of your energy will return. The next day, you'll be the river again (or a beautifully polished stone). Both are great.

— Letting go of fears and anxieties, so you can truly flow —

To flow is to live in a space of deep and continuous trust that, once entered, we truly want to stay in. It's living in alignment, in the fullest, highest and deepest meaning of the word. And yes, of course, it's so possible for you to create in your life.

I know many of us find it so hard to let go of the need to control; but the idea that we can control things is only a perception. Thinking we can control things (and getting upset when we realise we can't) can hold us back from enjoying where we are right now, even if on a mental level you think zooming ahead is helping your dreams come true more quickly.

— Tap into the river's energy —

A little while ago, we spoke about how we can never step into the same river twice. To embody this, we can see that surrendering to where we are can be the source of flow.

Surrendering to where we are is about releasing fears and anxieties and stepping into the river anyway, trusting it'll take you where you need to be. Instead of constantly trying to swim upstream, let go and flow. Use your energy to take aligned action along the path the river is taking you, instead of investing all your energy into trying to go in a different direction, one that is against the current of your life.

See what I did there? You could take 'current' to mean the direction of the river's flow ... or as in currently or present time. Where are you currently in your life? Can you let yourself flow from here to where you need to be (even if you don't know where you'll end up), instead of fighting and forcing and strongarming your situation?

When you lean into the river of the unknown, you become who you were meant to be, while you figure out who you are.

Our inner critic is loudest when we feel uncertain; but that doesn't mean we have to listen. Our fear keeps us stuck firmly in our place, but how has anyone ever grown by not moving forward? (Except for, like, a tree?)

Our greatest challenges—even if that's all encompassed by the idea of leaning into uncertainty—help us to redefine what our passions are, and what our purpose is. If you never step into the river, you might never find out who you are, and what you're made of.

— Affirmations for embracing uncertainty —
— I give myself full permission to flow with my life
— I now step into my flow
— I am 100 percent ready, willing and able to flow with my life
— It's okay for things to feel uncertain

— I trust I'll receive the answers when I need to

— I trust I'm 100 percent in my flow

— I trust I know how to flow

— It's safe for me to flow

— I am ready to flow

— I allow flow to become my natural state of being, trusting that it is

— I am 100 percent ready, willing and able to flow with momentum again

— Finding your flow and momentum —

When things seem stagnant, finding our flow again can feel impossible. When I think back to that period of my life where I felt so stuck, I remember feeling exhausted by trying to find flow and open up to it again. I knew what it felt like—I'd been in flow for so long beforehand!—but I found that the more I tried to force flow to come to me, the further away I felt from it. I felt frustrated that I was 'doing' all the right things, that I was putting in so much effort, and that it so often felt like nothing I did made any ripples, like I was shouting out into the void and not even getting an echo back.

I see this differently now. I see that it's this sense of impossibility that has to shift first, for us to open to new waves of possibility, abundance, joy and flow.

And even though it felt like it took months for me to find my flow, after that period of stagnation and bewilderment when it felt like I'd ruined everything, I did find it again—a new flow—and you'll find yours again too.

When I had truly forgiven myself, when I had truly surrendered to what had transpired through my trying, and my failure, and when I took action from that space of truth and grounded energy and possibility, that's when I found flow again.

Initially, as I felt the flow come back, I was scared I would then do something to jinx it, that I would fail again and lose it all. And that's when a beloved mentor of mine said to me: 'Stay in your flow and things will continue to move towards you.' This is still on a post-it on my computer, and I look at it daily.

What was the one thing that helped me find my flow again? It wasn't one, it was many things, and of course I'm writing about all of those tools and mindset shifts here. But one of the biggest things was coming back to myself, coming back to trusting myself, my inner guide, my higher self, my guidance, and on top of all of that, getting out of my head, getting into my body, and trusting my own energy, direction, purpose and vision again.

I was done with self-pity, with resignation and with fear of failure. I was done with it. I wanted to get off the bench and get back into the game—my life. I didn't want to miss out, just because I was scared it might not work out how I wanted it to. In truth, things had already not worked out how I'd wanted them to, and I was still okay.

I wanted to feel the beautiful, pure and buzzing sense of possibility that envelops you when you start a new project, or plan an adventure, or do something that your soul is yearning for. I wanted to craft my life again, instead of sitting back and waiting for momentum to find me.

I want you to want all of that for yourself. I can't want it for you (although I do). I can't make you want it for yourself. And I certainly can't make you do anything about it. That's up to you. If your fire has been put out, **you** have to light it again. You have to step right up, and get your eyes on that ball again. If you're not ready quite yet, tune in. Why aren't you ready? What have you not done yet that might help you be ready? What are you waiting for?

I'm a softy at heart, I am. But I will get riled up about this, because it is a pivotal moment for you. This is when you build your resilience and look your fear in the eye and decide to rise. This is when you say: 'I get it. Something out of my control happened to me but I am okay, and I forgive myself and for how I reacted, but now I'm ready ... now I'm back, now I will rise.'

What's your inner dialogue right now? What do you need to tell yourself or remind yourself, to help you get back in the game? It's time.

— Clearing old momentum —

Sometimes when I leave a room in our apartment, I'll automatically reach to flick the light off, even if it's already off. I'm in such a habit of turning the lights off when I leave the room, that I don't even realise I haven't turned them on.

To create new momentum in our lives, we must let go of the old. Is there something you're doing on autopilot that you don't need to do anymore? Bring your attention to your everyday tasks and thoughts. What is old? What is not serving you? How could you be more mindful and conscious of making space for the new to show up?

— Where do you find your momentum? —

I know that for me, momentum came from the small things. Mostly, it came from acknowledging where there was already momentum in my life. I also created it by daily movement, mostly by walking.

To get some momentum back in my life (even if it was just to soothe my conscious mind), I started walking. I would literally give myself a gold star (stuck on a wall calendar) for every day I went for a walk. I needed to physically move myself forwards, instead of feeling like I was staying stuck. I would put on a Podcast or some music and just walk, every day, for thirty to sixty minutes. It not only lifted my mood and focus, but I also found that the more and more I went for daily walks, the more I tuned into flow and momentum. In fact, as I typed the initial words for this paragraph, I was on a walk! As I relaxed into movement, more sections of my book started to download into my consciousness while I was walking. So I opened a 'Spark file' I keep on my phone for moments exactly like this, and I started typing. Inspiration for your next move can hit you anytime, so make space for it, move towards it, and open up to it.

Why not create a new healthy habit of moving your body every day, to bring momentum back into your life too? If anything, it'll also give you a clearer headspace, increase your mood, calm anxiety, and help get some energy moving again.

Flowing affirmation

I open up to the natural flow of my life. I know
how to find my flow and stay in it. I know it's
safe to flow, and I am ready to flow.

chapter 32

SYNCHRONICITY AND
SERENDIPITY

———

The more we tune into flow, the more we invite synchronicity (events happening at the same time that have, to use psychiatrist Carl Jung's terms, *meaningful coincidences*) and serendipity (events happening by chance, in a happy, positive way) into our lives.

In real time as I write this, I've recently come back from an Australia-wide book tour for *You Are Enough*. That tour was something I didn't think I'd go on until about seven weeks before it began. Several months before the tour was even an idea, I'd been approached by no less than five different people and companies who wanted to hire me to speak at events or collaborate on speaking engagements with them, all within the same month. I couldn't see how I would be able to fit all these events into one month, but I trusted it would all work out, and I felt really excited by all of them.

Over a period of just a few weeks, all of those events dropped off one by one; either the organiser changed their mind about the date, or decided they didn't want to progress past the idea stage. Either way, I went from thinking I would be speaking at five events, to having no events booked in at all.

I could have felt flat, but instead I felt an expansion, a spaciousness, and excitement bubbling up. I could now see how I could plan my own events. I could now see that this month was to be my book tour month. Had those other five events gone ahead, I wouldn't have had the space to go on book tour. The other events had been the catalyst—they had shown me what I had to do, and also shown me I had to do it for myself.

So I got to work organising a four-city tour, which quickly expanded to a six-city tour by popular demand. I organised the main details of the whole tour in about ten days (I work fast!), announced it to my audience, and started the tour seven weeks later. It was brilliant and wonderful and I loved it all. I'm so happy those initial five events failed to eventuate, because by doing so, I had the most wonderful experience that I couldn't have foreseen just weeks before. Moral of the story: things might fail, and that might be the best outcome of all.

But not only that, there were so many tiny moments of serendipity throughout the tour too. Like the time I stepped out of the airport in Melbourne saying to myself: 'I wish I'd organised a car to pick me up.' No sooner had I finished the thought than a limo driver approached me and asked if I needed a driver, as his client's flight had been delayed. 'Oh yes, I do need a car, thank you very much.'

— You can't force it —

Serendipity is such a beautiful thing. We can miss it if we're not looking at the spaces in between, if we're only looking at where we think we've failed.

Serendipity is life's flow, when you are fully in it.

We can't force synchronicity and serendipity, we can only open up to them once we've forgiven ourselves and cleared our energy, once we've decided we're worthy of being supported and of receiving our dreams, or something better.

Synchronicity and serendipity affirmation

I notice the synchronicity and serendipity in my life and welcome them by embracing flow and trust in my life.

TRUST YOU'LL GET THERE, OR SOMEWHERE

BETTER, ALL IN GOOD TIME.

———

#itsallgoodbook

chapter 33

BE HERE NOW

———

*H*ands up if you're a patient person! ... Anyone? Ha, jokes aside, tuning into patience actually becomes easier when we are in our flow, because trusting and flowing naturally means we lose the urge to rush, and to worry about the future.

We don't need to rush the present moment when we're content, grounded and settled where we are (while also continuing to move towards our goals and dreams without rigid expectations).

We don't need to worry about the future or the outcome when we trust we'll be able to meet it, no matter what it is.

Tapping into patience also helps us in the process of surrendering. It's really an incredibly important element in the process of surrendering. It's also much easier to do once we've committed to letting go, and to relinquishing the need to control things.

We can't control the timing of our lives, so we have to let that one go. Instead, we must trust ourselves, our path, and the timing of our lives.

I think that trying to rush yourself through a difficult period can make it seem longer, more arduous and more painful. Even though I've had times where I've tried to brush past my feelings, I've still always known that if you're feeling something now—pain, heartache, grief, anger, rage, sadness— it's best to let yourself feel all of it now.

Don't hide it away, don't shut it down, and don't suppress it. Surrender to it, to let it pass. Feel it all now, and do what you need to do to acknowledge it, to honour it and to clear it. If you're feeling the sense to rush, what else could that mean for you? I think I used to try and rush through what I was going through, because I wasn't fully accepting myself in the situation. I wanted to rush so I didn't have to really see what I was going through, and because I didn't know how I'd get through it or what the outcome would be.

Rushing felt like a way to bypass the healing … but the universe had other plans for me. I had to feel it all, in order to heal. Only then could I find my flow again.

If you let yourself feel it all now, the perceived need to rush through it will drift away. And by letting go of your need to control, you'll probably move through it faster anyway.

If you allow yourself to be present, to not rush, you'll see that you'll be given everything you need to manage a situation when you need it, even if you can't see it happening on your own schedule. Give it space to happen in its own time, with you being fully present, and let this be true for you: it will happen when it's meant to, as it's meant to, or something better will fill its space.

What happens if the 'something better' isn't what you expected? That's okay too. You're still on the right path. You surrendered to where you were, you allowed the flow of life to carry you, and you are resilient enough to continue to show up to your life. What you desire can still flow to you, even if the timing isn't matching what you so carefully planned. Trust this: let it happen in its own time. Show up fully to it, accept it, see it and be in it.

Then let it go, and allow patience to become a word that slips into your mind, body and spirit, as a way of soothing and saying: 'It's all good. Everything will be okay.'

— It wasn't working, until it worked —

I couldn't rush what I was going through, when I went through my months of healing, grief, frustration, sadness and anger. I had to be in it, and every time I tried to rush it away, I found myself feeling more out of alignment than if I had just stayed in the discomfort (teaching me that being in discomfort didn't necessarily mean I was out of alignment!).

Staying in alignment started to feel hard and exhausting. But with this came something wonderful: I changed my mind about what alignment meant. I learnt that you can be in alignment (flow, integrity and synchronicity) and in discomfort (challenges, growth and integration) at the same time.

Being in alignment didn't mean that everything was perfect in my life, and that there were no hurdles. It meant that (among so many other beautiful things) I could easily cope with whatever flowed to me; and more than just 'cope'—I could thrive through it and beyond it, staying in integrity and alignment with who I am and what I was creating, and receiving, in my life.

When I grounded myself in that space, truth and energy, when I completely surrendered to where I was by being okay with being there, by not trying to rush the time away, by being patient and trusting in the timing of my life and my lessons, by showing up for myself again (and not fearing failure in the process), I found my flow again. I forgave myself on an even deeper level. I trusted on an even deeper level.

Staying in alignment started to feel even easier for me. Again, I let go of something: of the idea that being in alignment was something I 'had to do', another chore or task to tick off my list. It became something that invited in more ease and flow. By doing so, the cycle of alignment, flow, trust and synchronicity became my home ground again.

— It just wasn't happening —

The process of writing this book made me tune into trust and patience more too. Several months ago, before I'd written even half of this book, I decided that once I'd finished the first draft, I'd take myself to Byron Bay for a solo writing and editing retreat. I'd done this for *You Are Enough*, and it was one of the best things I could have done. It made space for clarity and productivity (and in fact, it's up there with one of the best experiences of my life, because it was such a dream for me to be able to do that).

So I looked through my calendar, months in advance, to try and find a three to four-day gap that would work. I couldn't find one at all. Between everything else I had going on in my life, finding time for this quick little writing retreat just wasn't happening, and I started to feel quite disheartened. I thought perhaps I'd just book myself into a hotel for a weekend and have a little working 'stay-cation,' but even that was looking dismal.

So I let it go, and lo and behold, four things soon became crystal clear:

1. My timing was off because, as the universe would have it, I would not be finishing my second book when I initially planned. Instead I'd be going on my book tour for my first book.
2. If I had forced the timing it would have been terrible, as I would have felt rushed and off kilter. In fact, I probably would have had to cancel the trip, which would have felt awful to me. (Or, if I'd forced it, I wouldn't have been ready for the trip, which would have also felt awful!)
3. I actually wasn't ready to finish the book at that time; I was still integrating some of the lessons I had to write about. And since this book is so much about surrender and trust, I had to … um, surrender and trust myself!
4. Once I let go of the desire to control the timing, it all worked out beautifully. I could book a little solo writing retreat in Byron Bay between two writing workshops I was holding—the perfect way to practise what I preach. (I'm here right now, as I type this to you, and it's heavenly!)

— The present day is okay —

To rush is to wish time away, and why would we want to do that? Ah, I hear you; if you're going through a rough time, or if you want to see the answer before the answer is ready for you to see it, how great if you could just rush through it! Sorry, no can do. Trying to rush through hard times can make them feel ickier, harder and longer in duration.

Be here now, in the good and the bad, and surrender to the unknown. Allow yourself to trust in your ability to manage whatever flows to you, knowing you are more than capable, knowing that the discomfort of impatience doesn't need to last and it can, in fact, be an arrow directing you to where you need to be. And trust you'll get there, or somewhere better, all in good time.

When you can open up to patience, to trust, and to a commitment to ground yourself in the present moment, you can stay focused and committed to yourself, and to your dreams. Ah, exhale!

Patience affirmation

I now open up to patience, to being trusting, content, grounded and peaceful in this present moment. I trust that it is safe for me to be patient, and to be here, now.

chapter 34

THE LOVE STORY OF
YOU AND YOU

———

*I may not have gone where I intended to go, but
I think I have ended up where I intended to be.*

DOUGLAS ADAMS

*I*f you haven't ended up where you intended to go,
why not decide that, instead, it's exactly where you're
meant to be? Why not see your unexpected destination as
an exploration into who you really are, taking you where
you're really meant to be?

Now, where are we in the journey of this book? You've
forgiven yourself, you've let go, you've surrendered, you've
recalibrated and aligned and dreamed, you're trusting and
patient. And now, you must keep exploring.

You must keep exploring who you are, and what you love,
and how you want to be, and keep showing up for yourself and
your loved ones. You now know that it's so necessary and so
okay to let go of old ways of being, thinking, attaching and
attracting, in order to explore the new, and you know how
to let go of fears around this.

Now take what we're about to go through as a gentle reminder that it's okay to explore what you love again, and to visualise a beautiful, positive future, in spite of past adversities or perceived failures. This is more than dreaming and setting new goals, as you may have done by now. This is about reconnecting with yourself in a greater way; this is about rekindling the love story of you, and you. Cute!

— You're not lost —

I was recently driving home from a group fitness class and I found myself behind a hired campervan, which had big, bold spray-painted letters on the back that read: *I'm not lost ... I'm exploring.* I thought that was brilliant. This was just a few days out from me sitting down to edit the book, so the timing of this sign was absolutely perfect.

Imagine if, during a time of feeling lost, ungrounded or overwhelmed, you saw it as an exploration? Imagine what you might discover about yourself, your life, and your desires ... if you focused on discovery and exploration, instead of loss and defeat.

We know our disappointments and failures are often the catalysts for our greatest change, our greatest growth, and our greatest journey. They create new maps for us to follow, new signposts for us to notice, and they can spark new life into old, tired ways of doing things. Perhaps for you, it's time to explore new options, new experiences, new opportunities and new mindsets.

Perhaps your latest failure will turn out to be the best thing that's ever happened to you.

— A playful restart —

Tuning into a more playful energy will help you explore new options for moving forwards, because bringing joy and lightness into our lives helps us to forget about the mental aspects of our journey and to simply enjoy it for what it is.

When I felt myself truly coming out of my 'surrender shell,' I felt daily rushes of pure energy and delight at even the most simple and mundane things. My life felt lighter, and I felt happier.

Here are some questions and activities to help you to begin, again.

— If you shifted your focus from feeling lost to exploration, what might you discover?

— What does your new roadmap look and feel like? Where do you want to be heading in your life?

— What could you do to bring more lightness, fun, playfulness and creativity into your life? When can you do it?

— What have you always wanted to do, that you haven't felt capable of doing before? Is anything stopping you from doing it now?

— What do you truly wish to do again? When you can you do it?

Exploration affirmation

I am open to exploring new dreams and desires, and to bringing more lightness, play, ease, joy and fun into my life.

chapter 35

GOING INWARDS

———

*G*oing inwards, making time for self-care and indulging yourself can be a road map, a pathway, and a route back to feeling whole. I say 'route back to feeling whole' because I want you to know that you are already whole. You might just need a reminder, and self-compassion through indulgence might be that support you crave.

I used to find two ideas came to mind when I thought about indulgence: the first was the idea of self-care, and the second involved things that were guilt-inducing, things that felt selfish, or things that felt so far away, like white sandy beaches on exotic, private islands.

Now I understand indulgence to be much more like self-compassion at the highest level—self-care that is a level above what you might be used to. It's an honouring of who you are and what you need; it's saying 'no' when you want and need to; it's a deep listening to what your mind, body and spirit really need; a deep call to heal in a way that feels good for you; and a deep allowing to let yourself do what you need to do to integrate, to give and receive, and to rise up again.

Hopefully, after reading this chapter, you allow yourself to nourish and self-care and set boundaries for yourself, on a level you might not have seen in your life yet. You don't have to feel guilty for this; but I understand that you might initially. That's okay; you can let that guilt go, with self-permission for self-compassion. Ah, see how lovely it is to be gentle with ourselves?

You must understand this: feeling guilty for indulgence, especially indulgence after you've been through a tough experience or a challenging time, won't help you feel healed or whole faster. But ... self-compassion will. Give yourself permission to indulge or self-care or self-love (word it however you like), as a way to heal.

When you give yourself permission to indulge, you won't be procrastinating anymore (like those times you want to do something for yourself, but first you do the laundry), and you won't be holding grudges against yourself. You'll be listening to your soul and fine-tuning how you relate to yourself, how you heal yourself, how you love yourself, and how you protect your energy. It's a beautiful thing and it'll stay with you long after you release your self-imposed grudges because of your self-defined failures on your self-defined timelines.

Deep self-care and indulgence might mean spending money on yourself, but it doesn't necessarily mean buying things or doing things (although a fresh mani and a bouncy blow dry can only help!). It can also be a way of being; of going slower, inwards, and of being gentler to yourself, of setting boundaries and of honouring them.

There's really no right or wrong way to indulge in self-care, as it's such a personal thing. Just honour whatever you feel you need to do. For me lately, I've been loving lying on my bed on a Friday afternoon (or on the weekend) with my journal or a notebook, a cup of Earl Grey and a book (and sometimes, a few shows on Netflix!) and letting myself just lie down for a while. Just lying down ... revolutionary!

I begin by just closing my eyes and breathing—a meditation with no time limit or stimulus. With nothing to do and no expectations placed on myself, I feel my entire body sink into a relaxed state. This helps me show up in a more mindful and conscious way in my life. It's so simple, but I find it so powerful. When was the last time you just closed your eyes and breathed for a while?

Remember, you don't need to spend money to indulge to heal; it might be a slow afternoon in the park with some music in your ears and the sunshine on your skin, or a sleep-in, or a night at home, or whatever else feels really, deeply, truly nourishing and indulgent to you.

The most important part of using self-care, self-compassion and indulgence as a way of healing is to ask yourself what you really want and need, and then allow yourself to create it, make space for it, and receive it. It's not just you who will benefit from this; the people you love will love the more contented, grounded, calmer version of you too.

— Indulging to heal —

Indulging to heal can look like many things:

— Setting boundaries that suit the new you, that actually serve and support you (as in saying 'no' to things that are outside of what you can manage beautifully right now, and feeling more than okay to do that)

— Taking time out of your everyday life or out of work to simply rest, without any guilt

— Lazy couch days with a good book and a big mug of tea or coffee

— Buying beautiful natural and organic skincare, make-up and body care products, to use on yourself as a daily act of self-love

— Buying some gorgeous candles for your home, and some beautiful essential oils to diffuse or use to make your own perfumes and massage oils

— Lazy afternoons in bed with a marathon of your favourite shows and more mugs of tea

— Going at a much, much slower pace for a little while

— Having more rest and deep sleep

— Sitting down for meditation when it feels good for you; or making time and space to lie down with your eyes closed—with no stimulus, no noise, light or music—just you and your breath

— Getting some energetic healing or bodywork: kinesiology, reiki, massage, acupuncture, reflexology, a facial etc.

— Booking a little retreat or getaway with friends, family, your partner, or solo

Indulgence as healing affirmation

I give myself full permission to indulge in what I need right now. I am allowed to care for myself, love myself and give myself compassion as I heal.

chapter 36

PLUGGING INTO YOUR POWER

Once you come back from failure—and if you've truly integrated the lessons and recalibrated from the experience—you'll find your sense of intuition may be incredibly heightened.

Now you'll find you can tune into and use your personal power on a different level. You are more aware of what works for you in your life, what you will and won't accept, and where you want to invest your time, thoughts and energy.

After a failure, you can actually align to feel even more confident in your life, in your goal setting, and in your process of living in flow. That is why plugging into your power is a key pillar in surrendering, trusting and flowing.

— Doing the inner work (without making it feel like work) —

When we do what comes most naturally to us, we restore the natural order of our world—the world within us. What might that look like? Well, it's whatever feels most natural to you; whatever you feel most whole doing. Chances are that while you're healing from a failure, you're not doing it as much as you'd like to.

This is how we do the inner work without making it feel like work: by taking stock of what lights us up; by aligning to what makes us feel whole; and by doing the things that come most naturally to us, to restore the natural order of our innermost world.

What lights you up? What makes you feel whole? What comes naturally to you? Are you doing enough of it?

— Activating your personal power —

You are more powerful than you know, and even if things in your life have felt like they're not going your way, this doesn't mean you are powerless. This doesn't mean you are doing something wrong, and that everyone else is doing something right. It doesn't mean it's time for you to throw the towel in and walk away from everything you've been building (unless, of course, you've decided to change your mind from a space of awareness and compassion).

Activating your personal power will help you release overthinking, because you know that whatever the outcome, you're strong and resilient enough to manage it beautifully. When you're standing firmly in your power, you can look for the best of yourself in every situation. You stop being a victim. That can be hard to hear, I know, but it's time to play bigger and stand up for yourself and what you want to create in your life again, no matter how tough times may have been for you recently. You can trust that positive change is possible, hence allowing it to be possible for you.

It's time to activate your personal power. To enable this, we'll now go through how you can use a variety of intentions, affirmations and meditations as tools.

When I consider the difference between intentions and affirmations, I think of it like this: an intention is a way of activating our personal power and it's an energy we can embody, almost like a personal mantra. An affirmation is something we work with in a different way, as a reminder to tune back into our intention. (This is a really personal definition, so if it doesn't resonate with you, feel free to leave it in this chapter. If it works for you, take it with you into your life.)

Personal power intentions

— It's my intention to step fully into my personal power and create the life I dream of
— It's my intention to love, forgive and heal myself, so I can move forward fully, and in my flow

Add your own intention/s in now (give yourself space to start activating your personal power yourself!):

_____

_____

_____

Personal power affirmations

I now step into my personal power

I know how to step into my personal power

I know how to activate my personal power

I am 100 percent in my power

It is safe for me to be powerful

Add your own affirmation/s here:

_____

_____

_____

Personal power mini meditation

I now activate my personal power.

It's safe for me to be powerful.

I have clear and healthy boundaries that allow me
to activate and protect my personal power with
ease and flow, with grace and compassion.

Tuning into my personal power allows me to let go of the fear
of failure and the fear of change. It allows me to let go of the
fear of my anxiety, and of the anxiety and fears themselves.

I am powerful, I am strong, and I am capable.

Knowing this helps me flow.

Tuning into this helps me manifest.

Believing this helps me back myself.

I am powerful.

I am strong.

I am capable.

---

chapter 37

OR SOMETHING BETTER?

My perception of what it means to 'manifest' is constantly growing and evolving. The more I learn about myself, about my ability to focus on a goal, clear blocks around achieving it, open up to create it and receive it (or not receive it, because something else was needed, something else came to fill its space) and then make space to hold that dream, whatever it's final outcome, the more I learn about manifesting, making space to receive reciprocity and abundance.

I believe that manifesting is about opening up to receive what is—on some level—already meant to be received by us. But I also believe it's about taking clear, aligned and inspired action to draw in what we desire.

When we manifest something we desire in our lives, it's because we're already capable of creating it and receiving it.

And when we don't manifest what we desire, we have to trust we'll be okay anyway (because we will be).

We can't force manifestation, and we can't force receiving. When we believe we're worthy of manifesting, creating what we desire (or something better), letting go of outcomes and expectations along the way, and when we know that we're capable of receiving and holding what we've created, that's when we truly feel in our power. That's when we can take action to create and open up to receive.

I think there's a level (or several) of synchronicity and divinity contained within the energies and powers of manifesting, and I also think there's always space to open up to create and receive new wonderful things through intention and action.

Of course, as we've already discussed, we have free will. Hence we have the ability to construct new pathways that once stood upon, guide us even further towards manifesting and receiving what we desire (and what—on some level—is already meant to be received by us).

So when we manifest, we're opening up to our divine potential and saying, 'I'm ready to receive this or something better.' Then, we're taking action to bring our desires into reality. Sometimes the 'taking action' is undertaking steps to bring our dreams to fruition; sometimes it's the 'action' of setting the intention, clearing blocks to receiving, and then letting it go.

I think manifestation is a little bit magical, but I also don't think it has to be this unattainable thing that you can't have access to unless you have the Secret Special Golden Fairy Sparkling Unicorn Dust.

We **can** make decisions, set goals, take aligned action, clear blocks and invite in what we desire.

But we can't control the process, and we have to be okay with the very real possibility that we may not receive what we want to manifest. This doesn't make you a failure. It's life. But guess what? New wonderful things await you, and not receiving what you desire can sometimes be the greatest gift of all.

— What does it mean to manifest? —

As I mentioned, I have an ever-deepening understanding of manifesting. To me, it's not simply about the surface level stuff of asking for more money and finding some on the street as you walk into your favourite cafe (although, that's a lovely thing to find!), but also about creating a life that feels really good to you. It's about trusting in yourself to take action to make your dreams come true. It's about being resourceful in bringing your dreams to life, while being mindful about what you want to create and receive in your life. And it's absolutely about believing you're worthy of receiving.

Manifesting has so many layers, all of which we need to be clear on, if we're to create what we truly desire (or something different, or something better).

As I began writing this chapter, I received a strong intuitive hit: *Use the word 'creation' alongside 'manifestation'. In this chapter, they can be one and the same.* And this feels so true.

If I were to create 'manifestation' as an equation (which is really funny as I hated maths at school), it would look something like this:

creation + receiving – expectations = manifestation

Sometimes on our manifesting journeys, we get lost in the creation stage or the receiving phase. Very often, we get lost in the expectations stage. Your inner duty—your commitment to yourself—is to honour and love and open up to all three: creation plus receiving, with a little—or a lot of—letting go on the side.

Let's go through the layers of manifesting now, looking at them as a lens through which we can see where we need to add something helpful (more trust?) or subtract something stagnant (less expectations?). I believe the layers can be interchangeable (hmm, except maybe for the first point—you'll see what I mean), and for each piece of a puzzle that you manifest, you may lean into more layers or less. It's about energy and vibration; so tune into what feels right for you.

— Knowing you are worthy —

Fully opening up to manifest what we want (especially after we've come back from failure or disappointment) is to believe we're worthy of receiving it.

If you actually manifested what you desired, how would you feel? Would you believe you're worthy of receiving it, or would you sabotage yourself in some way?

If a friend were to arrive at your doorstep with a gift right now, for absolutely no reason, how would you feel? Would you push it back and say you don't need it or deserve it? Would you lose it, or break it by accident? Would you think you owe them something in return? Would you then buy them two gifts in return, to really make up for them extending a gift to you in the first place? Or would you simply allow yourself to receive it, and thank your friend?

This is about doing the inner work first. Your first step is to believe you're deeply worthy of receiving what you desire. How can you receive anything, if you don't believe you're worthy of it?

Trust in your own innate worth first. Trust in your ability to set a goal, take action, make space, and then receive it. Trust that you can manifest, create and receive.

Affirmations to work with:
— I trust I can manifest, create and receive
— I believe in myself
— I trust my manifesting abilities
— I believe I can receive what I desire (or something better)
— I trust in the energy of my manifesting power
— I believe I can create a beautiful life for myself

— Clarity and creation —
This stage is your dreams in their raw state. Think of this as clarity-filled and clarity-fuelled dreaming. You are clear on what you want and what you're working towards, and you feel energised and in flow to make it happen.

Be specific with your intentions and clear in your awareness. What do you really want to manifest? When do you want to manifest it by? What will it mean, if you manifest this? What negative thoughts are holding you back from receiving it? Get clear on those questions first, then allow yourself to receive, receive, receive.

Affirmations to work with:
— I have a clear vision of my future
— I know what I'm working towards

— I am clear on my goals
— My goal is …
— I am aligned to …
— I am working towards …
— I tune into the energy and vibration of what I desire
— I know how I want to feel, as I work towards my dreams and goals

— Receiving and flowing —

This is where you set your intention for what you want, and start to become aware of how you can make space for it to be received and held in your inner (and outer) universe. Think of this as setting an intention to open up to receive, and then allow yourself to receive it.

Affirmations to work with:

— I am worthy of receiving what I desire, or something better
— I am 100 percent ready, willing and able to make space for my dreams to manifest
— I am 100 percent ready, willing and able to receive and flow

— Taking action —

Now take action. What can you do, in order to create what you desire? This isn't about being in a constant state of hustle, but about taking action in a way that feels good and right for you; and trusting that when you take aligned action from a space of trust, and in flow, you are helping your dreams come true.

Affirmations to work with:

— I easily take aligned action to help bring my dreams to fruition
— I know how to take action
— I trust I am doing enough
— I take action in a way that feels good to me

— Letting go of expectations —

You know those times you go searching for the perfect outfit for an occasion, and you find absolutely nothing, and then the next week you're rushing out to the shops to grab milk, and you walk past the most perfect dress you've ever seen? You weren't looking for it, or even expecting it to come, yet it found you in the spaces in between your yearning. This is a simple example of the power of manifesting, once we've let go of controlling the outcome.

We've gone through releasing expectations all through this book, so this is where you put your new knowledge and gained wisdom into play. There are so many ways we can manifest and receive what we desire, and letting go of our expectations around how and when our dreams will materialise or manifest is what helps us do this.

While we can take beautiful actions to manifest and receive, we can't manifest on our own time; we must trust in divine timing too. We must trust and surrender to the bigger plan. When we can own this and honour this, that's when we can manifest what we desire, create what we need, and receive what is ours—or something better—at the right time, and not a moment sooner.

We might also not receive what we wanted to manifest, and this is perfectly okay too.

Set your goals, and then let them go, so they (or something better) can rush in to fill the space you've created for them, when your dreams are ready. You don't have to fight so hard to open up to create and receive what you want. The easiest way not to fight is to let it go. If it doesn't come through for you, it's not meant to be yours yet, or at least in this state, or perhaps ever. And that is more than okay; trust there's something else awaiting you.

Affirmations to work with:

— I allow my dreams to manifest in a way that supports my highest good
— It's safe and easy for me to let go
— I release the need to control the outcome
— I open up to flow
— I am in my flow
— I tune into flow
— It's safe and easy for me to flow with my life

— Making space to receive —

Making space to receive can be practical, such as opening up a new bank account to put away some savings or cleaning out your desk; it can be spiritual, such as through meditation to create more headspace; it can be emotional, such as letting go of friendships or relationships that feel cluttered and heavy; or it can be physical, such as becoming more intentional with the foods you're eating, how you're moving your body and what products you're using on your skin, as well as making your home and workspace more beautiful, decluttered and inviting.

Let go of what you no longer want or need in your life, let go of what's not longer working, and invite in what you truly desire.

Affirmations to work with:

— I make space to receive

— I have space to receive

— I know how to make space to receive

— It's safe and easy for me to make space to receive

— Believing in co-creation —

Please don't think that manifesting is up to you alone. You are co-creating your life with a higher, divine power. Remembering this will allow you to trust so much more in your power and ability to manifest what you desire. You're not doing this alone; you are supported.

Affirmations to work with:

— I know I am supported

— I believe in the power of co-creating my dreams

— I trust I am always supported, as I co-create my dreams

— I trust my dreams and goals are coming to me at the right time and in the right form, when I am ready

— Appreciation and gratitude —

To maintain your inner power in what you are creating and allowing into your life, you must appreciate and acknowledge what has already come into your life.

Like that time I'd been on my way to my car to go and grab a coffee, having been feeling a bit stressed about money, and then found a very squashed fifty cent coin in my driveway that other people had obviously been stepping over. Of course, fifty cents wasn't going to buy me a coffee, but I picked it up, allowed myself to feel grateful for it, put it in my wallet and acknowledged it as part of the abundance all around me.

I also think we notice things more when we're looking out for them. If you start to acknowledge and be grateful for finding a coin on the street, you may find them more often.

Affirmations to work with:

— I am grateful for what I've already co-created in my life
— I am grateful for where I am right now
— I notice the abundance all around me
— I acknowledge and appreciate all the abundance in my life

— Let it come to you —

When we manifest what we desire, we are in flow, in alignment and tuned into the magic that is synchronicity in our lives. To manifest with ease is to be in alignment with our goals and dreams, with our yin energies and feminine flow.

But I think it's time we took the pressure off ourselves and what we're wanting to manifest. Just like the best things in life are not always the expected things, I think we sometimes get so stuck in our ways of what we **want** to manifest that we close our eyes and energy to the magic and wonder of what we are **meant** to receive and manifest.

Manifesting is surrendering to what you want, and allowing it to come to you when the time is right (if it's meant to). If you attach to what you want, but don't get it, what happens? This is when you can feel disappointment, anger, resentment and bitterness, lack of self-confidence, fear and even fist-shaking rage. How much better would it feel if, before you attached, you let go, softened and surrendered?

Affirmations to work with:

— I manifest with ease
— It's safe for me to let go in order to receive
— I tune into the magic of manifestation

— Manifestation by design —

We can also manifest by pure design: as in deciding something isn't working for us in our lives, making space for what we want to create, and then taking aligned action—actually filling the space with what we do want.

Since my husband I moved into our apartment over five years ago, one corner of our bedroom held a beautiful teak chest, handpainted in a deep teal, and a TV hung on the wall above it. It was a lovely little spot, but the thing is, we barely ever turned the TV on, and I didn't really need the extra storage space. In other words, the chest was storing things I probably could have let go of, and often became the dumping ground for things I was going to 'put away tomorrow.'

For a little while, I'd been decluttering and beautifying our home—cleaning out cupboards, upgrading things in our home, buying beautiful indoor plants, and generally making our home feel even nicer to be in. (I'd also been spending time making new boards on Pinterest, and I had whole boards dedicated to interior design, which I called *Reading Nooks* and *Home Inspo* and *A Room of My Own*.)

One Sunday morning, I looked at the TV on the wall and the chest in the corner, then decided that I wanted to make better use of that space—I wanted to create a reading nook.

Inspired by Marie Kondo's book, *The Life-Changing Magic of Tidying,* Nic and I both realised this little corner was not bringing us joy. So Nic took the TV off the wall, and I put the chest and the TV up for sale online.

I had no idea when the pieces would sell, but I already knew what I wanted to fill the space with: a comfy armchair, a footstool, a throw, a little side table, some art prints for the wall, and one of my new indoor plants (a Zanzibar gem in a marble pot, on a copper pot stand). I wanted a space I could relax in, read in, write in, and drink tea in—a space that not only felt light, spacious and calm, but that also created and held more lightness, spaciousness and calm in our home. So I set out to do just that.

I went to one of my favourite furniture and homeware stores to look for an armchair I'd seen online. When I got there, they didn't have the one I'd spotted online but they did have one in a better shape and size. It was also on sale, and available for me to take home that day. So I purchased it, stuffed it in the boot of my car, and drove home with the biggest smile on my face.

That night, a friend of a friend got in touch to purchase the chest (she'd seen me mention it on my social media profiles), and I ended up selling it for exactly the same price as my new armchair. And, after Nic told his parents we were selling the TV, they decided they'd buy it, so off it went to them the next day.

I found the throw I wanted (beautiful creamy cotton, handmade, with woollen tassels in cream and black) as well as the side table (a simple wooden one), a cool little footstool, and some gorgeous new linen cushion covers to spruce up some old cushions we already had. Plus, the company I bought the throw and cushion covers from added in four mugs, as a gift with purchase.

The following week, I added a beautiful macramé wall hanging into the mix and some art prints. So within a week, I'd created my new reading nook.

As I sat down in my reading (and Netflix!) nook the next Sunday afternoon, just a week after I'd decided to create it (when I'd had no idea how it would all unfold, or when it would all happen), I took a few deep breaths in and out. I sunk into the chair, put my feet up on the footstool, put my tea on the table, and looked around at what I'd created. I felt ridiculously proud of myself.

Not a day goes by that I don't sit in that nook and let myself exhale from the day.

Not a day goes by that I don't look at that nook and remind myself what I can create.

Not a day goes by that I don't see the nook and feel immense gratitude for how it all panned out.

It might be 'just' a little reading nook, a little corner of our bedroom, an armchair ... but to me it's representative of so much more. To me, my little reading nook represents desire becoming reality, action turning into manifestation, making space to breathe and receive, and allowing things to unfold in their own way (without force, but with action).

To make space for this little nook, I had to let go of things I no longer needed or loved. The decluttering in and of itself was wonderful, but investing time and energy into my intention was the real prize.

And even though my little reading nook was mostly by design (with some serendipity and co-creation interwoven throughout), that's still creation; that's still allowing yourself to receive; that's still manifesting.

And in fact, the more we manifest by design in our lives, the more we live in alignment, hence the more we can truly manifest and receive what we desire (or something better).

(And yes, I let Nic sit in the reading nook too. Sometimes.)

— What do you really want? —

I had a client who was putting her all into her business for many moons, and she felt like she wasn't getting anywhere. She invested time, money and so much energy and intention into what she thought she wanted—what she thought she should want—and after a couple of sessions of business alignment coaching, she realised she had been trying to fit a square peg into a round hole.

As soon as she switched on to what she truly wanted, she realised she had been doing things back to front: trying to manifest an outcome based on an idea that didn't fit her, instead of working with the energies of what did fit her, to manifest an outcome with more ease, grace and synchronicity. Within a week, she felt the full force of beautiful flow come whooshing back into her business and life. Opportunities presented themselves, she felt more financially supported and she realised that following **her** dreams was what mattered— not the dreams she thought she should want.

Sometimes, if we put lots of energy into manifesting what we want, and it doesn't happen the way we want it to, we can feel defeated and let down, as if we'd done something wrong. But this is where we must let go of the expectations we hold around the form in which our manifestation will come to us. This is when we must become crystal clear on what we actually want.

We can't always choose what it will look like, or when it'll arrive. And the beauty of this is that when we're in a space of flow, alignment and trust, it doesn't even matter! The timing becomes synchronistic, the outcome matches us where we're at.

Let's take some of the masculine (yang) analytic mindset out of the feminine (yin) receptive process of manifesting. Yes, we need both of these energies—we need to take action **and** open up to receive—but we can't analyse the manifesting process. It's a little bit of magic, and a lot of pure intention, and it's bigger than our minds. So, let it go.

Tune into flow, tune into alignment, tune into trust. Take action in a way that truly serves you and be all here, so that what you need to manifest will arrive at the right time for you.

Some questions worth exploring:
— What am I hoping to manifest and receive in the next little while?
— What negative thoughts come up around manifesting this?
— Do I believe I'm worthy of manifesting and receiving this? Why/why not?
— What can I be/do/say to myself/believe to remind myself that I am worthy of receiving what I desire, or something better?
— Are there any actions I can take towards making this come true?

— Is there an energy I can embody to support me being in flow, and to help make this come true for me? (For example, tuning into surrendering and trusting more)
— If I receive what I want, how do I think I'll feel?
— If I don't receive what I want, in my timeline, what will I allow myself to feel and know?

The greatest takeaways from this chapter on manifesting are this: let yourself dream; take aligned action to create and make space for what you want; and then stay in your flow, so you don't attach to it, in order for you to open up to receive what you desire, or something better.

chapter 38

DANCE WITH CHANGE

———

To be our best in this life, we must dance with change. We must explore the depths and heights of our potential and our reality by trusting ourselves, taking aligned action (that sometimes feels like taking risks), and releasing our attachments to our expectations of how things should go.

We must listen to our hearts and our intuition, clear and balance our energy and lean into our flow.

We must move to the beat of the song that's playing in our lives today, and not to the song that was playing a month ago, or a year ago, or a decade ago.

If the floor feels like it's spinning beneath your feet, spin with it, and you won't fall over. And then when that song is over, get up, wipe the sweat from your brow and dance to the next song. Do it with a smile, with passion and a deep devotion to your dreams, and with a sense of reverence towards yourself, towards your life, and towards all the experiences that have brought you right here, right now.

Dance with change affirmation

I let myself move and flow and dance with change.
I trust myself, my path, my guidance and my decisions.
I know I am supported, and on the right path. I trust
and surrender to the bigger plan for my life.

YOUR STORY ISN'T WRITTEN IN STONE;

IT'S WRITTEN IN THE STARS—WITH FREE

WILL AND SYNCHRONICITY, WITH

INTENTION AND ACTION.

#itsallgoodbook

chapter 39

THIS IS YOUR JOURNEY, AFTER ALL

'Gratitude' wasn't a word that always resonated with me. Sometimes it felt forced—almost like if I couldn't use it to improve my mood, then I had failed at a key component of personal development.

The truth is that gratitude didn't always change my mood when I felt down, but other things that are so connected to appreciation and acknowledgment did: like softening into myself and being kinder to myself; the feeling of community and connection and laughing with my family and friends; and taking a few moments out of my day to spend time by myself in a cafe or in nature. All of these things tap into the energy of gratitude, without it having to be something that I felt I had to force myself to feel.

Now though, I feel so differently towards the word 'gratitude.' Now, it plugs me back into my flow and fine-tunes me for my constant evolution and expansion. It's not necessarily about me sitting down to write a 'gratitude list'—it's more about me closing my eyes and tuning into the energy of what I have, so I can continue to align to what I am already bringing in, through being in flow.

— **In a space of gratitude** —

What does it feel like when you are in a space of gratitude?
— I am grateful for ...
— Gratitude feels like ...
— I tune into gratitude by ...

While this concluding chapter will help you call in the energies of being grateful, I invite you to name it whatever you want. Appreciation? Acknowledgement? Thankfulness? Grace? You can choose—this is your journey, after all.

With gratitude for where you've been, you can now move forwards, using the lessons contained in this book, and the insights that may have flowed to you through the reading of this book.

Trusting, surrendering and flowing are mindsets and intentions that help energise us, activate our personal power and support us. They are not something we 'get to' and then drop.

One tiny change can mean so much.

In Seth Godin's words: *As soon as we realise that there is a difference between right now and what might happen next, we can move ourselves to the posture of possibility, to the self-fulfilling engine of optimism.* That quote is balm to my soul.

Take that truth and let it simmer under the surface, then seep into every part of your being. Because the truth can change, your situation can change, your story can change. You are not stagnant. You are not stuck. You are not still. You are forever changing, growing, evolving, expanding, clearing and progressing. You are consistently finding your path, and staying on it (even when it feels confusing).

With time, and with intention and inner healing work, we can be grateful for the disappointments and the failures we've experienced. They may have sent you down a path you couldn't have expected, but deeply needed to experience.

To be grateful for the disappointments means we're also celebrating the wins and achievements that came afterwards, when we rose through the failure and the fire, the pain and the confusion, and when we opened our hearts, minds and eyes again, finally seeing clarity, truth and trust.

Life is better when we trust, surrender and flow. I know it as well as I know that the sweet sticky chai that I just brewed on the stove is sitting on my desk. I know it as well as I know that the beautiful lychee and peony candle I just lit is burning a hot flame next to me. I know it as well as I know that I was meant to write this book now, not last year, and not next year; and I know it as well as I know you were supposed to read it now, not last year, and not next year. (Although you can definitely read it again next year!)

Now is the time for us to be here; now is the time for us to trust. Now is the time for us to believe in ourselves and to back ourselves, to explore the heights and depths of our potential and our lives, and to give ourselves a break, if we think we fail a little along the way. The failure in and of itself is not what counts; it's the lessons contained within the experience and the way we then recommit to ourselves, our dreams, our goals, our potential and our life purpose that counts.

You are always moving forwards, even when it feels as though you've gone backwards, even if the ground beneath your feet feels shaky and unstable, even if you can't see your future or where you're going.

You can rewrite your story, even when it feels as though it's been written in stone.

Your story isn't written in stone; it's written in the stars—with free will and synchronicity, with intention and action.

You can accept the situation, then forgive it, surrender to it, and then change how you feel about it. You can do all that and so much more, because you trust (and know, and believe) that **it's all good; you can trust and surrender to the bigger plan.**

It's all Good

COMPENDIUM

*U*se the table on the following spread as a ready reference for all those feels that you sometimes don't know how to manage. I've included a list of common emotional states we go through during and after a failure, the subsequent emotions relating to a period of integration and up-levelling, and some of the energetic tools you may find useful.

I've recommended crystals you may like to work with, as well as specific Bach Flower essences. These are quite easy to find worldwide, and beautifully supportive for clearing and calming emotional states. (Do an online search for 'Bach Flower Essences' or pop into your local health food store. A lot of pharmacies stock them too.) I've also listed some affirmations and a few other tools and suggestions that may help.

After the table, you'll see I've given you space to add in any other emotional states you often feel, and the tools you know support you. Knowing how to serve and support yourself—with compassion and love and gentleness—will be one of your greatest companions along this journey of surrendering to where you are, so that you can more fluidly and effortlessly move to where you want to be. Understanding your needs, and what will calm and soothe you, is as important as me offering this table up to you.

Emotional state	Crystal	Bach flower essence
Anger	Angelite for peace and calm	Holly
Comparison	Rose quartz for self-love and compassion	Larch and/or Holly
Exhausted and burnt out	Hematite for grounding; moonstone for flowing with natural cycles	Centaury, Olive, Wild Rose and/or Willow
Fear or panic	Red jasper, hematite and sodalite for grounding	Aspen, Mimulus, Rock Rose and/or Star of Bethlehem
Feeling stuck in your head	Rose quartz to bring you back to your heart	Clematis
Impatience	Aragonite for patience and grounding	Impatiens
Lack mentality	Citrine for abundance	Chicory, Gorse and/or Heather
Lack of clarity	Clear quartz and iolite for clarity	Scleranthus and/or Wild Oat
Loss of passion and joy	Peridot for joy	Hornbeam
Overwhelmed	Aquamarine for simplification	Elm
Procrastinating	Carnelian for action and creativity	Scleranthus
Sad and lost	Amethyst for clarity, Peridot for joy	Mustard, Gorse and/or Hornbeam
Stuck, lacking momentum	Chrysoprase for movement and action	Gorse and/or Rock Water
Stuck in old patterns	Green calcite for letting go	Chestnut Bud Flower, Gentian and/or Pine

Affirmation	Other
I let go of all I no longer need; calm is within me	Move some energy; go for a walk or a run; meditate
I am enough; I am doing enough and I am on the right path for me	Read my book, *You Are Enough* (joking, not joking)
I call my energy back to me	What do you need to do to restore your energy levels? Give yourself time to rest and restore deeply
I ground my energy in the now; I am safe	Do some alternate nostril breathing and/or exercise to calm your mind
I come back into my body and ground my thoughts and energy in the present moment	Focus your thoughts and energy through intention, breath, exercise, journaling and meditation
I am exactly where I need to be right now	Go for a run; move your body; focus on the present moment
I have everything I need right now	Focus on what you do have; what is enough for you right now?
I allow myself to be guided by my intuition; I know what to do next	Tune into patience; take aligned action and don't rush things; allow clarity to come to you
I refresh, restore and clear my energy, and open up to the energies of joy and inspiration	Explore things you love: new things, old things, forgotten things. Find joy in the simple and everyday things
I let myself simplify, and I know what to focus on first	Go to yoga; go for a walk; have a nap; do a big brainstorm of everything that's on your mind to let it go
I know I am capable and I take action today	Believe in yourself; clear your schedule and sit down to do what you need to do
I see clearly and know I'm exactly where I'm supposed to be	Sit, breathe and ask your highest self: 'What do I do next?'
I invite in flow and flow with my life again	Create movement and momentum in your life; go for daily walks outside
I allow myself to let go of all I no longer need, knowing I can create healthy new patterns	Give yourself permission to change, and believe you can! Be patient and compassionate

Your turn. Add your own in here:

Emotional state   **What I can do to support myself**

_____

_____

_____

_____

_____

_____

It's all Good
RECAPPED

It's all good.

Own your story.

Liberate your expectations.

Be proud.

Stay open to magic, synchronicity and flow.

You are the master.

You can shift your perception.

Your failure is your progression.

See your strength and resilience.

Keep the golden nugget.

Forgive.

Let go.

Accept.

Surrender.

Heal.

See things in a new light.

You can work it out on the way.

Recalibrate.

Integrate.

It's crystal clear now.

Lead from your heart.

Dream again.

Allow yourself to change.

Be compassionate.

Up-level.

Stand on new ground.

Be seen.

Trust.

You are safe.

Receive.

Flow.

Move with synchronicity and serendipity.

Be patient.

Explore.

Indulge in self-care.

Stand in your power.

Manifest … or something better.

Dance with change.

Be grateful.

It's all good.

A NOTE TO MY READER

I have an interesting story to tell you. Just after I finished the first draft of this book, I realised it was the right time to let my big, beautiful, bold project go, to close it all down. Yes, the one that was the catalyst for this book, the one that helped me go to new heights because of the challenges, the lessons, the experience; the one that I dreamed about for so long, worked on so hard, and loved so much.

I realised it was time to let it go because as much as I still loved that dream, goal and project, it no longer fitted in with who I am anymore, or where I'm going. It's not that it was completely out of alignment with me—it's just that it began to feel like it was in alignment with a previous version of me. To make space for the new, I had to let it go.

The second that this decision came to me, in a flurry of writing and brainstorming and journaling, of opening up to guidance and letting go of attachments, I felt a huge wave of relief rush through me—release and lightness, clarity and gratitude.

I felt the bitter sweetness of failure, the delightfulness of clarity, the rush of new beginnings and the gratitude of rebirths.

I felt it all and more, and it made such perfect, divine sense. I'd been through a challenging period, I grew from it, I became stronger because of it, I wrote about it and shared it in the container of this book, and then … I let it go.

Is there something—something else, something that hasn't yet come through to you in all the words and phrases and pages of this book—that you see you can (or must, or want to) let go of now too?

Whatever it is, trust that it's safe for you to let go of. Trust that when you let go and make space, something will rush in to fill it. You don't always get to choose what that is. But you do get to choose to make space, be yourself, show up, and to allow yourself to create and then receive what you desire … or something even better.

Love,

Cass x

CONNECT WITH CASS

I'd love for us to stay in touch. For more support in trusting yourself and your path in life and business, visit my website at www.cassiemendozajones.com for books, articles, meditations, online courses, events, free resources and more.

You'll also find me on social media:

Instagram.com/cassiemendozajones
Facebook.com/cassiemendozajones
Pinterest.com/cmendozajones
Twitter.com/cmendozajones

#itsallgoodbook

ACKNOWLEDGMENTS

Thank you so much to Leon, Rosie, Errin and the entire Hay House team. I'm so honoured and grateful to be part of the family. Thank you for backing me and supporting me with this book.

Thank you so much to my wonderful designer and friend, Dani Hunt, for another epic and beautiful book cover. You created a cover that epitomises flow, trust and surrender. I love it, and I'm so grateful.

Thank you to my amazing clients who allowed me to share their stories throughout the pages of this book. And thank you to my wonderful readers and clients for your support. I'm beyond grateful for your presence. Thank you for being here.

Thank you to my beautiful extended family, family-in-law, friends and support team. I love you, and am so grateful for your constant love, encouragement and support.

And thanks to my amazing parents and sisters; thanks to Mum for sending that text about remembering how brave I'd been, thanks to Dad for the money chat (and all the delicious dinners) and to both of you for all your support always, and to my sisters for always being there for me. I love you.

And thank you to my hubby, for sending me off on my solo writing retreat and telling me to enjoy it all, even though I was in beautiful Byron Bay without you, and for reminding me that everything would be okay, on the days I'd well and truly forgotten. I love you.

ABOUT THE AUTHOR

© Bayleigh Vedelago

Cassie Mendoza-Jones is the author of the bestselling book *You Are Enough*, and a kinesiologist, business alignment coach, naturopath and speaker.

She works with women, and with entrepreneurs, healers, coaches and creatives who are driven, devoted and honouring their dreams, and who want to become more powerfully aligned to their bigger vision, clear away perfectionism, procrastination and overwhelm, and create their own version of a beautiful and aligned business and life.

Her lessons and insights have been featured in national and international publications such as *Collective Hub, body + soul, Women's Fitness* and *Australian Natural Health* magazines, and on popular websites such as ELLE, The Daily Guru, news.com.au, Vogue.com.au, Sporteluxe, marie claire and smh.com.au. She's spoken at events and workshops around Australia for a variety of companies such as BUPA, Barre Body, New Balance, LinkedIn, Morgan Stanley and Eat Fit Food, as well as at her own popular workshops and events.

Her work is for you, if you're ready to let go of limiting beliefs, fears and worrying thoughts that consume you, and if you want to build a life and business that feels really good to you.

www.cassiemendozajones.com

NOTES

NOTES

NOTES

NOTES

NOTES

NOTES

NOTES

NOTES

NOTES

NOTES

NOTES

NOTES

NOTES

NOTES

HAY HOUSE

Look within

Join the conversation about latest products, events, exclusive offers and more.

f Hay House UK

🐦 @HayHouseUK

📷 @hayhouseuk

💜 healyourlife.com

We'd love to hear from you!